plot, a multitude of facts, a wealth of philosophica
ts, and a huge number of comparisons and symbols. So co
it that experts have had trouble placing it in a liter
e, calling it a prose epic, a prose allegory, an extende
em, a symbolic romance, a romance of the sea, a metaphy
el, a psychological novel, a saga of the whale, and a tal
c adventure. Bu

Herman Melville:
Moby Dick and Other Works

sification says
plexity of Moby
alls this vast
a rich work of a

wealth of philosophical statements, and a huge numbe
risons and symbols. So complex is it that experts hav
ible placing it in a literary genre, calling it a pros
prose allegory, an extended prose poem, a symboli
a romance of the sea, a metaphysical novel, a psycholog
el, a saga of the whale, and a tale of tragic adventur
critic John D. Reeves points out, "no one classificatic
ugh—a shortfall that testifies to the vast complexity c
k." He, like many others, therefore, simply calls thi
k a "novel." Moby Dick, published in 1851, is a rich wor
ith an exciting plot, a multitude of facts, a wealth c
hical statements, and a huge number of comparisons an
So complex is it that experts have had trouble placin
literary genre, calling it a prose epic, a prose allegory
ded prose poem, a symbolic romance, a romance of the sea
ysical novel, a psychological novel, a saga of the whale
ale of tragic adventure. But, as critic John D. Reeve
ut, "no one classification says enough—a shortfall tha
s to the vast complexity of Moby Dick." He, like many oth
refore, simply calls this vast work a "novel." Moby Dick
d in 1851, is a rich work of art with an exciting plot,
le of facts, a wealth of philosophical statements, and
mber of comparisons and symbols. So complex is it tha
have had trouble placing it in a literary genre, callir
se epic, a prose allegory, an extended prose poem, a sy
nance, a romance of the sea, a metaphysical novel, a ps
al novel, a saga of the whale, and a tale of tragic adve
t, as critic John D. Reeves points out, "no one classif
ays enough—a shortfall that testifies to the vast co
of Moby Dick." He, like many others, therefore, simpl
is vast work a "novel." Moby Dick, published in 1851, is
k of art with an exciting plot, a multitude of facts

∽Writers and Their Works∾

Herman Melville:
Moby Dick and Other Works

RAYCHEL HAUGRUD REIFF

Marshall Cavendish
Benchmark
New York

Acknowledgments
Cyrus R. K. Patell
Associate Professor
Director of Undergraduate Honors
New York University

Marshall Cavendish Benchmark
99 White Plains Road
Tarrytown, NY 10591
www.marshallcavendish.us

All quotations are cited in the text. Additional information and sources are included
in the Notes section of this book.

Note on *Moby Dick*
The Oxford World Classic 1988 text of *Moby Dick*, edited by Tony Tanner, titles Melville's classic
as *Moby Dick*, not *Moby-Dick*, as Harrison Hayford and Hershel Parker did in their 1967 Norton
edition of the novel. Tanner claims that the Oxford edition "follows the American first edition of
1851, incorporating only those changes which it seems could only have been made by Melville."
(Tony Tanner, "Note on the Text," *Moby Dick*, p. xxvii) Since the newest research suggests that
Melville did not intend to use a hyphen, his novel in this book is written as *Moby Dick*.

All Internet sites were available and accurate when sent to press.

Library of Congress Cataloging-in-Publication Data

Reiff, Raychel Haugrud.
Herman Melville : Moby Dick and other works / by Raychel Haugrud Reiff.
p. cm. — (Writers and their works)
Summary: "A biography of writer Herman Melville that describes his era,
his major works--especially Moby Dick, his life, and the legacy of his
writing"—Provided by publisher.
Includes bibliographical references and index.
ISBN-13: 978-0-7614-2592-2
1. Melville, Herman, 1819-1891. 2. Novelists, American—19th
century—Biography. I. Title.
PS2386.H346 2007
813'.3—dc22

2006032673

Photo research by Linda Sykes Picture Research, Hilton Head, SC

The photographs in this book are used by permission and through the courtesy of:
Berkshire Atheneum Public Library, Pittsfield, MA: cover, 2; The Duncan Osborne Collection of
Herman Melville, A. Frank Smith, Jr. Library, Southwestern University: 8; The Granger Collection: 10,
11, 26, 33, 34, 36, 40, 42, 52; Bettmann/Corbis: 55; © 1930 by R.R. Donnelley & Sons, Inc. and
The Plattsburgh College Foundation, Inc. All rights reserved.: 57; Reproduced with the permission of
the Special Collections Library, The Pennsylvania State University Libraries: 61; Photofest: 90;
Museum of the City of New York/Corbis: 92; Columbia University Libraries: 102;
The Everett Collection: 104; The Kobal Collection: 112; Cover, Melville, Herman,
The Confidence Man, Copyright ©2003 The Modern Library, Paperback edition, Dix, Edwards &
Company: 116; Rare Books and Special Collections, Thomas Cooper Library,
University of South Carolina: 122.

Publisher: Michelle Bisson
Art Director: Anahid Hamparian
Series Designer: Sonia Chaghatzbanian

Printed in China
1 3 5 6 4 2

Contents

citing plot, a multitude of facts, a wealth of philosop
atements, and a huge number of comparisons and symbo.
mplex is it that experts have had trouble placing it in
rary genre, calling it a prose epic, a prose allegor
xtended prose poem, a symbolic romance, a romance of th
metaphysical novel, a psychological novel, a saga o
ale, and a tale of tragic adventure. But, as critic Jo
eves points out, "no one classification says enough—a s
ll that testifies to the vast complexity of Moby Dick."
ke many others, therefore, simply calls this vast w
ovel." Moby Dick, published in 1851, is a rich work o
th an exciting plot, a multitude of facts, a wealth of p
phical statements, and a huge number of comparisons and
ls. So complex is it that experts have had trouble placi
a literary genre, calling it a prose epic, a prose alle
extended prose poem, a symbolic romance, a romance o
a, a metaphysical novel, a psychological novel, a saga o
ale, and a tale of tragic adventure. But, as critic Jo
eves points out, "no one classification says enough—a s
ll that testifies to the vast complexity of Moby Dick."
ke many others, therefore, simply calls this vast wo
ovel." Moby Dick, published in 1851, is a rich work o
th an exciting plot, a multitude of facts, a wealth of p
phical statements, and a huge number of comparisons and
ls. So complex is it that experts have had trouble placi
a literary genre, calling it a prose epic, a prose alle
extended prose poem, a symbolic romance, a romance o
a, a metaphysical novel, a psychological novel, a saga o
ale, and a tale of tragic adventure. But, as critic Jo
eves points out, "no one classification says enough—a s
ll that testifies to the vast complexity of Moby Dick."
ke many others, therefore, simply calls this vast wo
ovel." Moby Dick, published in 1851, is a rich work o
th an exciting plot, a multitude of facts, a wealth of p
phical statements, and a huge number of comparisons and
ls. So complex is it that experts have had trouble placi
a literary genre, calling it a prose epic, a prose alle
extended prose poem, a symbolic romance, a romance o
a, a metaphysical novel, a psychological novel, a saga o
ale, and a tale of tragic adventure. But, as critic Jo
eves points out, "no one classification says enough—a s
ll that testifies to the vast complexity of Moby Dick.

Introduction

HERMAN MELVILLE (1819–1891) was an adventuresome young man who traveled in the wild American West; joined a merchant ship headed for England; sailed on the South Seas; hunted the most ferocious big game animal, the whale; lived as a prisoner with cannibals; and roamed though the Pacific Islands. When he was twenty-five, he returned to New York and began to write sea romances about his exciting times.

With the enormous success of his first books, *Typee* (1846) and *Omoo* (1847), Melville became famous as "the man who lived with cannibals." He wrote three more books, *Mardi* (1849), *Redburn* (1849), and *White-Jacket* (1850), before producing his masterpiece, *Moby Dick*, in 1851, a novel readers not only misunderstood but scorned. After publishing an even more unpopular book, *Pierre* (1852), Melville turned to short-story writing. Two more novels appeared in his lifetime: *Israel Potter* (1855), which was received with indifference, and *The Confidence-Man* (1857), which was condemned. With this failure, Melville gave up writing professionally. He and his family moved to New York City in 1863, where Melville spent nineteen years as a customs inspector (1866–1885) and wrote poetry.

When he died in 1891, his writing was practically forgotten. Since his rediscovery in the 1920s, Melville has been hailed as an American literary giant. *Moby Dick*, published in 1924, is regarded as a classic. Melville's works have been adapted into films, musicals, operas, and stage productions; the whale, "Moby Dick," is one of the most recognized literary icons. Melville is now recognized as one of America's greatest writers of all time.

My dear aunt

You asked me to write you a letter but I thought tht I could not write well enough before this. I now study Spelling, Arithmetic, Grammar, Geography, Reading, and Writing. I past a very pleasant vacation at Bristol. give my love to Grandmamma, Grandpapa, and all my aunts.

Your dear Nephew,
Herman Melvill.

THIS IS PROBABLY HERMAN MELVILLE'S FIRST LETTER, WRITTEN IN THE FALL OF 1828. THE NINE-YEAR-OLD TELLS HIS AUNT LUCY MELVILL THAT HE HAD NOT WRITTEN EARLIER BECAUSE HE FEARED HE "COULD NOT WRITE WELL ENOUGH." HE ALSO MENTIONS HIS SUMMER VACATION SPENT IN BRISTOL, RHODE ISLAND, WHERE HE VISITED HIS UNCLE, CAPTAIN JOHN D'WOLF, A WEALTHY SEAFARING MERCHANT AND ADVENTURER.

Chapter 1

The Life of Herman Melville

WHEN THE TWENTY-FIVE-YEAR-OLD sailor returned to New York in the fall of 1844, Herman Melville had not seen his family for almost four years. They were eager to hear about his travels, and he delighted them with exhilarating tales of whaling and of exotic South Sea islanders. One of their favorites was the thrilling story of his adventures while living with cannibals. Encouraged by them to write it down, he did, and thus began the writing career of Herman Melville—novelist, short-story writer, and poet. Since his books incorporate much of Melville's life experiences, the story of his life is especially fascinating, for, as biographer Lewis Mumford wrote, "In a great degree, Herman Melville's life and work were one" (4).

Growing Up

Herman Melville's life began quite fittingly for the author of sea novels. Born August 1, 1819, Herman lived in New York City near the Hudson River where ships came and went on the open ocean. His family was well-connected; both of Herman's grandfathers had been Revolutionary War heroes. An importer of French goods, his father, Allan Melvill (as the name was then spelled), provided comfortably for his family, repeatedly moving from each fashionable Manhattan location to an even finer one. Herman's mother, Maria Gansevoort Melvill, provided for their spiritual needs, baptizing her eight children (four boys and four girls) in the Dutch Reformed Church. As members of the upper class, Allan and Maria sent their sons to fashionable schools, where eight-year-old Herman

IN 1820, WHEN THIS PORTRAIT WAS PAINTED, BABY HERMAN'S TWENTY-NINE-YEAR-OLD MOTHER, MARIA GANSEVOORT MELVILL, LOOKED FORWARD TO A HAPPY, PROSPEROUS FUTURE. ONLY TWELVE YEARS LATER, HER LIFE DRASTICALLY CHANGED WHEN SHE BECAME A WIDOW. MARIA RAISED HER EIGHT CHILDREN BY HERSELF AND REMAINED A DOMINANT FORCE IN THEIR LIVES UNTIL HER DEATH IN 1871.

proved to be "the best Speaker in the introductory Department of the High School" (Metcalf, 9).

When Herman was ten or eleven, his father's business failed. Moving his family to Albany before creditors could find them, Allan tried to return to a happy life, enrolling his older boys in Albany Academy and setting up a fur business. But this also failed. By January 1832, Melville's father was exhausted, sick with pneumonia, and suffering from delirium, probably brought on by his terrible illness. So sick was he that his brother Thomas hoped "deranged" Allan would die, fearing "he would live, *a Maniac!*" (Parker, 1:58). When he died on January 28, he left his widow dependent on her wealthy relatives to support her because, at this time, women in New York State "could not own property or manage assets." (Robertson-Lorant, 54). Impoverished Maria changed the family's last name to "Melville," probably to try to get away from the stigma of being the bankrupt "Melvill" family (Leyda, 1:53).

The loss of his father changed Herman's life. In 1832, twelve-year-old Herman and his older brother, Gansevoort, were taken out of school and sent to work. From then on, Herman would be basically self-educated, except for some brief schooling in Albany and Lansingburgh. For

MELVILLE'S LOVING AND INDULGENT FATHER, ALLAN MELVILL, AN IMPORTER OF FANCY FOREIGN GOODS, LIVED BEYOND HIS MEANS AND WENT BANKRUPT IN 1830. IN JANUARY 1832, HE BECAME SICK WITH A FEVER AND DIED, LEAVING HIS WIFE AND EIGHT CHILDREN IN DISMAL FINANCIAL CIRCUMSTANCES.

the next seven years, young Herman worked as an errand boy at a bank; as a helper on his uncle Thomas Melvill's farm near Pittsfield, Massachusetts; as a part-time clerk in the brother's fur factory and store, which failed in 1837; and as a teacher near Pittsfield. To save money, Maria moved her family to Lansingburgh, a village ten miles north of Albany, in May 1838. Here, Herman took a course in engineering and surveying, hoping to get a job on the Erie Canal. However, when no job was available, the adventurous teenager went to sea.

Sailing

On June 5, 1939, Herman Melville's boyhood ended abruptly when he, now nineteen, set sail on his first sea voyage. For most of the next five years, this future writer, instead of receiving an advanced education, spent the majority of his time engaged in exhausting physical labor while "rubbing shoulders with the brutalized, exploited, and mostly illiterate seamen" (Arvin, 37). "His first voyage"—as he wrote in his subtitle of *Redburn*, the novel based on this experience—was on the merchant ship *St. Lawrence*, which was bound for Liverpool, where he worked in the humble capacity of "boy," washing decks and cleaning chicken coops and pigpens.

Returning home in early October, Herman found his mother entirely impoverished (Metcalf, 22) and immediately sought teaching jobs, securing temporary positions in Greenbush and later in Brunswick, New York. With no permanent job, in June 1840, the young man decided to seek his fortune in the American West at Galena, Illinois, where his Uncle Thomas had moved. However, his uncle was unable to help him, so he boarded a Mississippi steamboat, the setting for *The Confidence-Man*, and began the long trip home.

Restless, unable to secure a job, and, according to his granddaughter, probably disappointed in love (Metcalf, 23),

Herman once again decided to try life on the seas. On January 3, 1841, he sailed out of New Bedford, Massachusetts, on the whaling ship *Acushnet*, expecting to be gone three or four years, the usual length of whaling voyages. For the next eighteen months, the young man performed menial work on the ship, and he chased down and killed whales, facing death on the open seas. After harpooning a whale, Herman, like the rest of the crew, clung to the little open boat that rocked wildly from side to side as the whale towed it through the waters, and tried to avoid being speared by the lances and harpoons that were being flung about, or being maimed by the whizzing rope connected to the whale.

By July 9, 1842, finding life on board the whaler unendurable, Herman and his friend Richard Tobias (Toby) Greene deserted ship in the Marquesas Islands. For days, they climbed up and down mountains, while being pelted with torrential rain and suffering from hunger. To add to his troubles, Melville injured his leg, which he thought was bitten "by some venomous reptile" (Parker, 1:215). The two entered the valley of Taipi and lived for about a month among the cannibal inhabitants. Here young Herman enjoyed the relaxed social and sexual customs of the beautiful islanders, but worried that he might become a meal for his hosts/captors, a fear that grew greater after Toby made his escape and was not heard from again. This experience formed the basis of Melville's first book, *Typee*.

Herman escaped from the natives on August 9, joining the crew of the Australian whaler *Lucy Ann*, a far from ideal ship, with a sick captain, drunken first mate, wild crew, bad food, and poor sleeping quarters. When the whaler sailed to Tahiti in late September 1842, Melville joined the crew's mutiny and was briefly imprisoned. However, the supervision was so lax that Melville and his friend John B. Troy canoed to the nearby island of

Eimeo (now called Moorea) and worked as field laborers for a couple of weeks. These adventures form the plot of Melville's second novel, *Omoo.*

By November, Melville had joined the crew of the Nantucket whaler *Charles and Henry.* For the next six months, the ship sailed in the southern Pacific, the setting for Melville's third book, *Mardi.* When it anchored at Maui on May 2, 1843, Melville, who was free to depart because his contract was over, decided to quit whaling forever. Traveling to Honolulu, he worked briefly at a variety of odd jobs, including being a pin setter at a bowling alley.

On August 17, 1843, he enlisted on the navy frigate, the *United States,* scheduled to return to Boston. For the next fourteen months, Melville experienced the horrors of military punishment, being forced to witness more than 150 floggings (Parker, 1:262). Stripped to the waist, men were bound to the gratings and lashed by the whip until their backs were masses of blood and deep welts. Melville's condemnation of this punishment is found in *Mardi* and, decades later, in *Billy Budd.* By October 14, 1844, the *United States* had anchored in Boston, and twenty-five-year-old Herman Melville left the life of the sailor forever.

In his mother's Lansingburgh house, he delighted in entertaining his admiring family and friends with his sailor yarns. When they suggested that he write down his adventures in the South Seas, he readily agreed. Thus began a new chapter in Herman Melville's life. He declared to novelist Nathaniel Hawthorne some years later: "Until I was twenty-five, I had no development at all. From my twenty-fifth year I date my life" (Leyda, 1:189).

Writing for a Living

Melville spent the next twelve years, from fall 1844 to spring 1857, as a full-time writer. Working at a frantic pace, he produced nine novels (seven in the first seven years) and a number of short stories.

Typee: A Peep at Polynesian Life

Typee: A Peep at Polynesian Life, published in 1846, won instant appeal with its exotic setting and factual details. A racy book, *Typee* relates the exciting adventures of Melville and Toby after they deserted the whaling ship, their accidental arrival into the valley home of the Typee cannibals, their views and interpretations of the islanders' lives, their escapades with the uncivilized beauties, and their separate escapes.

When Melville submitted his novel to Harper & Brothers, the editors found the book interesting, but rejected it, stating that "it was impossible that it could be true and therefore was without real value" (quoted in Parker, 1:376). However, Herman's brother, Gansevoort, got the book published in Britain. He also was responsible for the American publication, showing it to the famous writer Washington Irving who, finding portions of the book "exquisite" and the style "graphic" (Leyda, 1: 202), sent the manuscript to his New York publisher. Because of Gansevoort's tireless efforts, *Typee* appeared in early 1846. Except for the religious press, which objected to Melville's comments on missionaries, the reviews were positive. Walt Whitman declared *Typee* a "strange, graceful, most readable book."

Melville was richly rewarded with this book, receiving recognition in his home country and in England, and gaining acceptance into the literary society of New York. One unexpected result of being the well-known author of *Typee* was that Melville became a sex symbol, desired by women and envied by men (Parker, 1:530).

In spite of the excitement over the novel, times were not completely joyful for Melville, whose brother, Gansevoort, died on May 12, 1846, less than two months after *Typee* appeared.

Omoo: A Narrative of Adventures in the South Seas
Harper & Brothers eagerly agreed to publish Melville's second work, *Omoo: A Narrative of Adventures in the South Seas,* a book Melville considered "a fitting successor to 'Typee'" by representing Polynesian life "as affected by intercourse with the whites" (Leyda, 1:233). With the exception of Melville's criticism of missionaries, this novel, which appeared in spring 1847, is comic and lighthearted. Loosely organized, it moves from one episode to another, beginning the day Melville escapes from the Typees to the day he signs on for another whaling voyage.

Because of Melville's negative portrayal of missionaries, the religious press, such as the *New-York Evangelist,* strenuously objected to the book; however, others appreciated it. The London *Spectator* declared *Omoo* "equal to its predecessor," while in America, Walt Whitman recommended it "as thorough entertainment—not so light as to be tossed aside for its flippancy, nor so profound as to be tiresome."

Mardi and the Voyage Thither
Melville promised his publisher that "If 'Omoo' succeeds I shall follow it up by something else, immediatly [sic]" (Leyda, 1:240). However, *Mardi* took longer to write than the author anticipated because other personal and professional matters occupied his time.

On August 4, 1847, twenty-eight-year-old Herman Melville married Elizabeth (Lizzie) Knapp Shaw, the "very happy and very, very good" (Robertson-Lorant, 153) daughter of Lemuel Shaw, chief justice of the Massachusetts Supreme Court, a friend of Herman's father and a family benefactor to whom Melville had dedicated *Typee.* Lizzie, who "was more down-to-earth than the vivacious 'belles of Lansingburgh'" (Robertson-Lorant, 152), enjoyed participating in serious conversations, reading poetry and novels, and examining ideas comprehensively.

Like Melville, she had a sense of humor. Because Melville was a celebrity heartthrob, cautious Lizzie, fearing a crowd would mob the church, arranged for a private ceremony at her home. The couple, famous but not financially well off, settled in New York City, sharing a large home with Herman's younger brother Allan and his new wife, plus their mother, four unmarried sisters, and little brother, Tom. The two older brothers were now the providers for this extended family. In this crowded house, Herman entertained friends, who found him "a right pleasant man to pass an evening with" (Metcalf, 43).

Professionally, Melville took on writing projects—reviewing nautical books for the *Literary World* and contributing satiric sketches on the Whig presidential candidate to *Yankee Doodle*. But mostly he labored on *Mardi*, writing "in his cold work-room wrapped in coat and shawl" (Metcalf, 56). The novel is a long Polynesian tale that begins realistically; turns into a wild romance of murder, blood-sacrifice, and chase; and is filled with philosophical reflections. Herman's sister Augusta and his wife copied the almost illegible manuscript to get it ready for publication, for Herman was notorious for bad penmanship and poor spelling (Delbanco, 35).

When *Mardi* appeared in 1849, most reviewers did not like the book, finding it a novel of "grotesqueness and prolixity" and advising Melville to return to subject matter he knew firsthand. Even Melville's wife did not understand the book, describing it as "the 'fogs' of Mardi" (Metcalf, 61). One person who did appreciate his efforts was the well-known American novelist Nathaniel Hawthorne, who proclaimed it "a rich book. . . . It is so good that one scarcely pardons the writer for not having brooded long over it, so as to make it a great deal better" (Metcalf, 90). Today, most readers regard *Mardi* as an interesting failure, recognizing that it "marked him for the first time as more than a writer of sea stories" (Metcalf, 43).

Financially, *Mardi* was unsuccessful, which was unfortunate since Melville now had a child to support in addition to his extended family. His first son, Malcolm, was born on February 16, 1849.

Redburn: His First Voyage

Melville reluctantly returned to writing narratives of personal experience, even though he wished "to write those sort of books [like Mardi] which are said to 'fail'" (Leyda, 1:316). In quick succession, he produced two books about his life on the sea: *Redburn* in late 1849 and *White-Jacket* four months later. He told his father-in-law, "They are two jobs, which I have done for money—being forced to it, as other men are to sawing wood. . . . my only desire for their 'success' (as it is called) springs from my pocket, & not from my heart" (Leyda, 1:316).

Redburn, based on Melville's first seagoing voyage, is the story of a naïve young man who boards a ship headed for Liverpool. He survives the harsh treatment on the ship and witnesses suicide, human hatred, and great poverty. By the time Redburn returns home, he has grown from a boy into a hardened, competent man.

Although Melville found *Redburn* a "beggarly" book and hoped he would "never write such a book again" (Metcalf, 71), reviewers did not agree with him, finding it "as perfect a specimen of the novel yarn as we ever read," and being "disposed to place a higher value upon this work than upon any of Mr. Melville's former productions."

White-Jacket; or, The World in a Man-of-War

The story of his experiences on the man-of-war ship appeared in America in March 1850. Even though *White-Jacket* was also written to make money, Melville criticized naval practices, particularly the floggings used on people who committed the smallest errors.

Hoping to sell *White-Jacket* at a good price to a British publisher, Melville tucked a copy of the novel into his luggage and sailed across the Atlantic in October 1849. His trip was successful, for he received £200 for the book (Leyda, 1:349). It was money well-earned because both British and American reviewers liked the book, enthusiastically praising it as "a creation of genius." The book was also successful politically, as Congress passed an act that banned flogging in the U.S. Navy.

Moby Dick; or, The Whale

After visiting Paris, Brussels, and the Rhineland, Germany, Melville sailed for home in late December, 1849, ready to write a novel about a young man who learns about life while whaling. In June 1850, he informed his English publisher that the book would be completed in the fall. But more than a year passed before the book was completed, and by then it had changed fundamentally.

Meanwhile, the thirty-year-old man decided to leave New York City to live more cheaply; in July 1850, he moved his family to Pittsfield, Massachusetts, and with his father-in-law's help, purchased a beautiful 160-acre farm in the Berkshire mountains that he named "Arrowhead" because of the flint arrowheads found on the property. Here the author lived for the next thirteen years, dividing his time between farm chores, such as feeding a horse and cow, cutting and splitting wood, mowing hay, and picking apples; literary composition, especially during the fall and winter months; and social activities with friends and relatives.

One outing with them was especially memorable. On August 5, 1850, Melville joined friends for a day-long expedition to Monument Mountain. Here he met Hawthorne. The two, who had taken shelter under some rocks during a thunder shower, instantly became friends—finding themselves kindred spirits—even though Hawthorne was fifteen years older than Melville. They visited often, and Melville was heartily welcomed to the Hawthorne home.

After getting to know Hawthorne, Melville began rewriting his whaling novel, giving it a new direction. All that fall, winter, and the next spring, he slaved on *Moby Dick*, shutting himself in his room immediately after breakfast and working until late afternoon. Although the room was drafty and cold, Melville must have enjoyed sitting at his desk writing about whaling, while periodically looking out the window directly in front of him to gaze on Mount Greylock which, to him, looked like a whale's back, and occasionally stirring his fire with a harpoon head. Although he based much of the novel on his own experiences, Melville added information gleaned from the factual writings of others—works on the whaling industry, whales, the white whale of the Pacific named Mocha Dick, and the destruction of the whale-ship *Essex* by a sperm whale. In addition, Melville read the works of creative authors such as Virgil, Shelley, and, in particular, Shakespeare. As he read and reread some of the Bard's great tragedies, he was convinced that he wanted to "write of real American life with a Shakespearean intensity" (Parker, 1:739).

By summer, *Moby Dick* was at the press, leaving Melville time to work on his farm, a necessary task because, as Melville lamented to Hawthorne, "Dollars damn me" (Metcalf, 108). He needed extra money to provide for a second son. Stanwix, named after the fort that Melville's maternal grandfather defended against the British during the Revolutionary War, was born on October 22, 1851.

At about the same time, *Moby Dick* appeared. Melville dedicated it to Nathaniel Hawthorne, to whom he wrote: "A sense of unspeakable security is in me this moment, on account of your having understood the book. I have written a wicked book, and feel spotless as the lamb" (Leyda, 1:435).

Moby Dick is Melville's masterpiece. Like Melville's other tales, the narrator is a novice, and his story is one of initiation. But Ahab is a tragic figure much like Shakespeare's great protagonists. In addition, Melville enriches his novel by including information about the activities that take place on a whaling ship, the history of the whale, and the use of the whale in myths, history, and art. Facts and storytelling meld together and form the basis for the imagery, metaphysical discussions, and comments that Melville includes in the book.

Although Melville knew *Moby Dick* was a great work, reviewers were not nearly as impressed. Even though some liked the elegant descriptions, the humor, and the originality, others condemned the novel's formlessness and irreverence. As a result, *Moby Dick*, which took Melville over a year and a half to write, was not a big success; his total earnings from American sales while alive came to $556.37 (about $17,000 in today's currency), much less than any of his earlier books (Delbanco, 178).

This monumental work almost destroyed Melville. According to his granddaughter, his "strength had been thoroughly depleted by the terrific creative strain of writing *Moby Dick*" (Metcalf, 135), and the poor reception so upset him that he went into a deep depression. So changed was Melville that his family and friends wondered whether he could ever be the same again. Biographer Newton Arvin asserts that "Melville survived by the scantiest margin. For the rest of his days he must have had the look of a man who . . . had been in the Underworld" (195).

Pierre; or, the Ambiguities

In spite of his exhaustion and depression, Melville threw himself into writing another novel to try to get enough money to feed his family, for they were poor and often hungry. By summer 1852, the new book appeared— *Pierre; or, the Ambiguities*, a work Melville assured his publisher was "calculated for popularity" (Metcalf, 135). But Melville was out of touch with his readers. *Pierre*, a psychological novel of passion, adultery, incest, murder, and suicide, was very unpopular with his contemporaries. Even twentieth-century readers complained that the book is filled with "some unexplained rage of the author's" (John Updike, quoted in Delbanco, 180). Most critics explain that Melville's "rage" came about because of the critically poor reception of *Moby Dick*; however, in 1948 author W. Somerset Maugham suggested that it was caused by his "disappointment with the married state" (quoted in Delbanco, 180) because Melville, Maugham believed, possessed sexual yearnings for males, an assertion which has not been proven. In spite of the fact that "Melville lived a heterosexual life" and did "not seem to have been actively homosexual" (Robertson-Lorant, 618), a number of gay critics (Delbanco, 204) have either hinted at or openly expressed their views that Melville was a homosexual. Thus, in the twentieth century, Herman Melville moved from being a heterosexual to a homosexual sex symbol.

No matter what the reason for Melville's rage, the reviews of *Pierre* were damning. It was labeled "trash of conception, execution, dialogue and sentiment," and condemned as "a dead failure, seeing that neither in design or execution does it merit praise." So shocked were critics that one headline screamed: "HERMAN MELVILLE CRAZY," while another reviewer alleged that Melville had "gone 'clean daft.'"

Pierre was a complete failure, so unpopular that it "destroyed for good his capacity to make a living as a writer" (Arvid, 198). Making Melville's financial matters worse, a fire at his publishers in 1853 destroyed the stock of his books.

In spite of these devastating blows, Melville did not wallow in self-pity. Instead he looked for a different way to support his wife, children, mother, and sisters. Since political appointments were often given to American writers at this time, Melville tried to secure a consular appointment in the South Seas. His family and friends worked hard to help him, for they had grown increasingly worried about his mental and physical health. Despite their efforts, he did not get the position, so Melville continued to write. With the birth of a daughter, Elizabeth (Bessie) on May 22, 1853, he had one more person to support.

The Piazza Tales

Melville turned to short-story writing, publishing more than a dozen stories and sketches from 1853 to 1856. *Putnam's Monthly Magazine*, paying Melville its highest rate, five dollars per page (Leyda, 1:481), published three of Melville's best loved short stories—"Bartleby, the Scrivener: A Story of Wall-Street" (1853), "The Encantadas, or Enchanted Isles" (1854), and "Benito Cereno" (1855). These three stories, together with "The Lightning-Rod Man" (1854), "The Bell-Tower" (1855), and an introductory story called "The Piazza" (1856), were collected and printed as *The Piazza Tales* in 1856. Generally, the reviewers found this collection "more uniformly excellent and more free from blemishes than any of Mr. Melville's later books." But, in spite of the good reviews, the book did not sell well.

Israel Potter: His Fifty Years of Exile

Another work published in *Putnam's* in 1854–1855 was *Israel Potter: His Fifty Years of Exile*, which also appeared in book form in 1855. It tells the story of a Revolutionary soldier who was a secret courier for Benjamin Franklin and a gardener for King George III before he disappeared and later returned to America. Very few reviews of *Israel Potter* were published, and those that appeared were short and bland. For instance, the *Boston Post* called it "an interesting book" but "not great, not remarkable"(in Parker, 2:248). With this indifferent reception, the book neither enhanced nor detracted from Melville's reputation; modern novelist and biographer Elizabeth Hardwick describes it as "an agreeable and readable book, not much read" (112).

In February 1855, just before *Israel Potter* appeared, Melville was laid up by an attack of sciatica and later by a flare-up of rheumatism, making him almost helpless for months. All spring, Lizzie cared for her physically disabled and mentally depressed husband, plus a new baby; Frances (Fanny) was born on March 2, 1855. By summer, Melville was somewhat recovered and able to entertain friends.

The Confidence-Man: His Masquerade
In spite of depression and physical ailments, Melville persevered with his writings, once again working on a book that was doomed to failure. *The Confidence-Man: His Masquerade* appeared in 1857. A thoroughly American book, its setting is derived from Melville's trip on the Mississippi riverboats where confidence men work from dawn to midnight. The reviews were varied. Some were complimentary: "curious, spirited, and well worth reading." Others expressed bewilderment: "You might, without sensible inconvenience, read it backwards." Still others were totally condemning: Melville "has not the slightest qualifications for a novelist." However, today the novel is praised for its "broad insights into the American psyche" (Delbanco, 248).

Traveling for Health
As Melville locked himself away in his study frantically writing one work after another, he became tense; for relief from his tightened muscles, Melville drank heavily, causing

him to become extremely irritable and touchy. Biographer Laurie Robertson-Lorant says that "Some family members blamed Herman's moodiness and poor health on his writing which was a convenient way of denying his growing dependence on alcohol" (370). His overuse of alcohol intensified his mood swings and made his depression greater. Although he was not actually "insane," as was rumored in later years (Mumford, 224), Melville was mentally ill, a sickness that today would be diagnosed as manic-depressive and treated with medication. But in the 1850s, no such illness was known, and Melville was left with no medical help to try to overcome his violent mood swings.

By 1856, he was in a "desperate" situation mentally, causing his family to suffer "from his bursts of nervous anger and attacks of morose conscience" (Metcalf, 159). They grew increasingly concerned that he would completely lose his sanity. On September 1, 1856, Judge Shaw, learning that his son-in-law "has been advised strongly, to break off the labor for some time & take a voyage or a journey & endeavor to recuperate" (Metcalf, 159), loaned Melville money so he could take an extended trip abroad.

Therefore, on October 11, 1856, Melville began a seven-month trip to Europe and the Holy Lands. In Liverpool, he reunited with Hawthorne, who had a consulate job there. Hawthorne immediately saw that his old friend was "a little paler, and perhaps a little sadder" (Leyda, 2:527–528), attributing part of Melville's melancholy to his spiritual desolation, as Melville struggled to either believe or not believe in God.

Throughout his trip, Melville remained depressed. The Greek islands he found "worn," "like life after enthusiasm is gone" (Parker, 2:310). The barren, stony Holy Land seemed sterile. Egypt and Italy were wearisome. In Rome, he wrote, "This day saw nothing, learned nothing, enjoyed nothing, but suffered something" (Leyda, 2:559). On May 5, 1857, he began his voyage home.

ELIZABETH (LIZZIE) KNAPP SHAW OF BOSTON MARRIED HERMAN MELVILLE IN 1847. SHE REMAINED DEVOTED TO HIM THROUGHOUT HER LIFE, BEARING HIM FOUR CHILDREN, HELPING HIM PREPARE HIS MANU-SCRIPTS FOR PUBLICATION, AND PRESERVING HIS UNPUBLISHED WORKS, INCLUDING *BILLY BUDD*, AFTER HIS DEATH.

Adding to his troubles was his precarious financial state. With the commercial failure of *The Confidence-Man*, which came out the month before he returned home, Melville worried about how he could provide for his family since, clearly, he could not make a living with his writings. *The Confidence-Man*, the last work of prose fiction that Melville published during his life, marks the end of his public literary career.

Lecturing

When Herman came home, he told his brother-in-law that he was "not going to write any more at present & wish[ed] to get a place in the N.Y. Custom House" (Parker 2:351). His family, fearing that if Melville returned to writing, he might "possibly become a confirmed invalid" (Leyda, 2: 567), worked hard to secure him this position, but their attempts were fruitless.

Therefore, Melville continued to look for "work that personal self-respect and fidelity to others demanded of him" (Arvin, 215). Two avenues were open to him: writing for magazines and lecturing. Since *Putnam's* was failing, Melville turned to lecturing. For three seasons, between 1857 and 1860, he went out as a traveling lecturer, talking on "Statues in Rome," "The South Seas," and "Traveling: Its Pleasure, Pains, and Profits." He was not very successful at this work, for in the three seasons, he "earned only $1,273.50, minus expenses" (Robertson-Lorant, 414), not sufficient funds to provide for his family. Generous Judge Shaw, as usual, supplemented the income.

Floundering

Melville's mental and physical health remained problematic. By 1860, the family was so worried that they encouraged him to sail around Cape Horn and across the Pacific with his younger brother, Tom, who was a sailor. From May to November, Melville traveled, but, homesick, he turned back in San Francisco, coming home still a sick man.

When he departed, he left behind a book of poems, asking Lizzie and Allan to get it published. Although they tried, no publisher was found, and the book was never printed.

As the years went by, Melville had no income except what little he earned on the farm. Once again he unsuccessfully attempted to get a consular post, even traveling to Washington, D.C., in March 1861 to try to secure one. That same month, Melville's benefactor, Judge Shaw, died. Although his father-in-law forgave the debts on Arrowhead, making the property Lizzie's inheritance, the family's financial burdens did not cease.

In spite of his disappointments, Melville's outlook on life improved somewhat in November 1862 after an accident, in which he was thrown from a wagon and suffered a serious injury. At the age of forty-three, he told his brother-in-law in December: "I begin to indulge in the pleasing idea that my life must needs be of some value," confessing that he once had "not care[d] to live very long" but now has "no serious, no insuperable objections to a respectable longevity" (Leyda, 2:656).

In fall 1863, having failed as a farmer, Melville traded Arrowhead for Allan Melville's Manhattan house, where he remained until he died. Although his health remained poor, patriotic Melville thought he might be able to get a naval appointment since the country was in the midst of a civil war, but nothing was available.

Some of his time was now spent writing poetry; Harper & Brothers published *Battle-Pieces and Aspects of the War* in August 1866. This book of more than seventy poems covers just about every important event of the Civil War: the battles at Antietam, Gettysburg, and Shiloh; Sherman's march through Georgia; and the surrender at Appomattox. For the most part, the reviews were not positive. Some critics did not like that he sympathized with people on both sides of the war; others condemned his writing style, calling his verses "little more than the rough ore of poetry." Of the 1,260 copies printed, only 551 were sold in 1866 (Leyda, 2:684).

Working as a Customs Inspector

The Job

Financial relief came on December 5,1866, when Melville finally got a government post. At age forty-seven, he began his only permanent paying job when he was appointed district inspector of customs at the New York harbor in the uptown pier near Harlem. His job was rather monotonous—working on the docks examining cargoes, superintending the unloading of goods, and reporting any violations of revenue laws. He was paid four dollars per day, making his yearly income $1,200, nearly as much as he earned in three winters of lecturing. He kept this job for nineteen years.

The family rejoiced that he had a permanent job. His mother reported that "Herman's health is much better since he has been compelled to go out daily to attend to his business" (Leyda, 2:686), while another relative noted that he was "less of a misanthrope" (Metcalf, 206).

Family Tragedies

Although Melville's wishes came true when he landed a government job, the family tensions which had been building for years did not lessen. According to biographer Robertson-Lorant, "Melville apparently compensated for feelings of powerlessness in his professional life by bullying his servants, wife, and children" (503). So bad was the home situation in early 1867 that Lizzie "was seen by family and friends to be living in a nightmare" because of her husband's ill treatment (Hardwick, 154). Exactly what this ill treatment consisted of is not clear, but many critics think Melville, drinking heavily, was physically abusive. So bad was home life that Lizzie, "convinced that her husband [was] insane" (Parker, 2:630), considered getting a separation from him, a drastic, almost unheard-of action in the 1860s. Although supported by her family and clergyman, she did not go through with the separation. For fortyfour years, she faithfully stayed by her husband's side.

Although Lizzie remained, the family fell apart. On September 11, 1867, the Melvilles' eighteen-year-old-son, Malcolm, died of a self-inflicted gunshot wound. Originally the coroner ruled it "Suicide . . . under temporary insanity of Mind" (Leyda, 2:688), but changed it a few days later to accidental death (Leyda, 2:690). Some speculate that Malcolm, a well-loved young man with a steady job, killed himself because of a quarrel with his father about his late night hours. Whether he purposely or accidentally shot himself with the gun he kept under his pillow (Leyda, 2:687), the Melvilles were devastated with the loss of their beloved son.

Two of their other children also caused Herman and Lizzie many worries. Stanwix became a wanderer, going to sea in 1869 (Metcalf, 212) and later trying a variety of occupations but failing at every one. Elizabeth (Bessie) developed rheumatism in the 1870s that crippled her, making her an invalid (Metcalf, 215).

With the deaths of family members—brother Allan, mother Maria, sister Augusta, and Lizzie's stepmother—there was no relief from stress and depression in the 1870s.

Clarel

Still a "'pondering man' to whom the mysteries of life presented an endless and imperious challenge" (Metcalf, 215), Melville began working on *Clarel: A Poem and Pilgrimage in the Holy Land*, a long verse novel of 18,000 lines meditating on the purpose of human existence. Privately printed at his uncle's expense in 1876, this "long, weary poem" (Mumford, 322) was not widely read or reviewed, and those critics who did review it, described it as "destitute of interest or metrical skill."

Lizzie was greatly relieved when *Clarel* was done, calling it a "dreadful *incubus* of a *book*" that "has undermined all our happiness" and caused her husband to be in "a frightfully nervous state" over which she felt the "gravest concern & anxiety" (Metcalf, 237). Melville's nervous condition continued long after the book was published.

Work-Related Problems

Part of Melville's suffering was a result of his frustrations with his work at the Custom House. His granddaughter says that this narrow existence caused her grandfather unhappiness, driving "him at times to desperate irascibility and the solace of brandy" (Metcalf, 215). As a result of his "irascibility," Melville was alienated from his family. In fact, his youngest daughter, Frances, who married Henry B. Thomas in 1880, seems to have harbored deep resentment towards her father all her life. Lewis Mumford, interviewing her in the 1920s, says that "only one condition limited that interview: on no account might I even mention her father's name" (quoted Delbanco, 180).

In spite of his frustrations, Melville wanted to keep his job at the Custom House because it gave him something to do and it provided a steady source of income. But the place was full of corrupt people, and workers were laid off frequently. Hardwick describes Melville's co-workers as "cannibals in woolen suits and ties and yet tattooed with ignorance and greed—some were arrested for embezzlement" (154). While other employees took bribes on the side, Melville "quietly declin[ed] offers of money for special services, quietly return[ed] money which ha[d] been thrust into his pocket behind his back, avoiding offence alike to the corrupting merchants and their clerks and runners" (Metcalf, 235). In all of his working years, Melville performed "his duties as to make the slightest censure, reprimand, or even reminder,—impossible from any superior" (Metcalf, 235). Because of his impeccable honesty and his irreproachable work, Melville's job was spared when two hundred customs employees were fired in 1877 (Arvin, 260).

In 1885, his job was again in jeopardy. On July 29, Lizzie, who regarded his work as a great blessing for both Melville and his family, feared that her husband might be laid off, "for which I should be very sorry as apart from every thing else the *occupation* is a great thing for him— and he could not take any other post that required head work, & sitting at a desk" (Leyda, 2:791). Once again, Melville kept his job.

At this time, the Melvilles' finances improved when Lizzie received inheritances from her aunt and her half brother, Lemuel Shaw Jr. Now financially stable, Melville was free to stop working. At the end of December 1885, Melville honorably retired at the age of sixty-two.

Less than two months later, new sorrow fell on the Melville family. In February 1886, their son Stanwix, age thirty-five, died in California.

Living in Retirement

Home Life

In the last few years of his life, Melville enjoyed his almost daily, fast-paced walks through the streets of New York. He also liked working in his "superb" rose garden, and delighted in "giving bouquets to his closest friends" (Hillway, 64).

Relationships with his family improved. He found much pleasure being in the company of his daughter Frances' young children, Eleanor and Frances, and they heartily enjoyed being with him, listening to his tales of wild adventures in faraway lands; going with him to Central Park to play, see the animals at the zoo, and ride in swan boats on the lake; and visiting his study to be treated to figs. Eleanor remembered the study as "a place of mystery and awe" (Metcalf, 283) and Frances recalled it as "such a wonderful place" with "no wall space at all, just books, books, books" (Parker, 2:908).

MELVILLE LOVED HIS FOUR CHILDREN AND MISSED THEM WHEN HE WAS AWAY FROM HOME. IN SPITE OF HIS AFFECTION FOR HIS CHILDREN, HE WAS OFTEN STERN AND DEMANDING.

During these retirement years, Melville took his last sea voyage, traveling to Bermuda in March 1888, returning by way of Florida.

Writings

Melville devoted much of his time to "leisured study, reading, and even writing" (Arvin, 288). In his last years, he wrote and privately printed two books of poetry. *John Marr*

HERMAN MELVILLE WAS AN IMPRESSIVE-LOOKING MAN EVEN IN 1885,
THE DATE OF THIS PHOTO, WHEN HE WAS IN HIS MID-SIXTIES. HE HAD
A THICK HEAD OF HAIR AND A MASSIVE BEARD WHICH HIS GRANDDAUGH-
TER ELEANOR LOVED TO SQUEEZE. SHE DESCRIBED HIS BEARD
AS "TIGHT CURLED LIKE THE HORSE HAIR BREAKING OUT OF OLD
UPHOLSTERED CHAIRS, FIRM AND WIRY TO THE GRASP, AND
SQUARELY CHOPPED."

and Other Sailors, 1888, is a combination of prose and verse; *Timoleon*, 1891, is a retelling of a Plutarch tale of a Greek who reestablished democracy at Corinth. As usual, Lizzie helped him prepare these books for publication. In love and gratitude, Melville inscribed one copy to Lizzie: "To Her—without whose assistance both manual and literary Timoleon &c [sic] could not have passed through the press—with her name I gratefully and affectionately inscribe this volume. Herman Melville. New York, June 1891" (Metcalf, 280).

Although these two works were Melville's final publications during his lifetime, his greatest achievement during these last years was the prose work *Billy Budd*, which he completed in April 1891. He also worked on a volume of poetry, *Weeds and Wildings Chiefly: with a Rose or Two*, which he dedicated to Lizzie. She stored these works, as well as his other unpublished writings, in a bread box. *Billy Budd* was published in 1924.

Death

On September 28, 1891, seventy-two-year-old Melville's heart failed. The cause was listed as "Cardiac dilatation, Mitral regurgitation. . . . Contributory Asthenia" (Parker, 2:920). In her memoirs, Lizzie wrote more simply: "He died on Sept. 28th 1891 after two years of failing health, induced partly by severe attacks of erysipelas terminating finally in enlargement of the heart" (Leyda, 2:836). His death made little or no impact on the literary world. In fact, many were surprised to read of his death because they had "long thought him dead" (Leyda, 2:836). So little was he remembered that the *Times* mistakenly recorded the death of "Henry Melville" while another publication called him "Hiram Melville" (Robertson-Lorant, 614). Melville was all but forgotten as a writer until a new generation brought his works back to life.

"OUR FIELD IS THE WORLD."

LIGHT DRAFT. SUPERIOR DESIGN.

CLEAN AND RAPID CUTTER.

McCormick Harvesting Machine Co., Chicago.

ESTABLISHED 1831.

McCORMICK HARVESTING MACHINE COMPANY AD, c1875.

AFTER THE CIVIL WAR, MASSES OF PEOPLE MOVED WESTWARD AND BEGAN FARMING LARGE PLOTS OF LAND. THE McCORMICK REAPER HELPED FARMERS HARVEST BIG FIELDS OF GRAIN MORE QUICKLY.

Chapter 2

Melville and His Times

MELVILLE'S YEARS WERE THRILLING times in America, both in the growth and direction of the country and in the development of literature. When Herman was nine, Andrew Jackson, an uneducated Democrat from Tennessee, was elected president, an event that is "one of the great landmarks in the evolution of American democracy" (Blair, et al., 82). With a common man in national politics, the country became more democratic.

Westward Expansion

When Melville was born in 1819, the nation consisted of twenty-two states covering most of the present United States as far west as the Mississippi River; when he died in 1891, it had doubled to forty-four, and it stretched from the Atlantic to the Pacific Ocean. Part of the reason the nation grew so rapidly is that many Americans embraced the doctrine of manifest destiny, the belief that the United States should control all of North America. As a result, there were conflicts with Mexico and Great Britain, which owned huge tracts of land.

In 1835, Americans in Texas revolted against Mexico, declaring Texas a sovereign nation. Ten years later, it became part of the United States. In 1846, Britain, not feeling it was worth the trouble to keep the Oregon territory, ceded it to the United States. After the Mexican War of 1846–1848, the United States obtained the southwestern territories—west from Texas to the Pacific, and north to Oregon. In 1853, America bought the strip of land that makes up southern Arizona and New Mexico in the Gadsden Purchase. Thus, by mid-century, the United States owned all of the lands making up present-day America, except Alaska and Hawaii.

Of course, people wanted to live in these newly acquired lands. In part, the westward movement was made possible by the Erie Canal, opened in 1825, which provided an easier access to the western lands. The discovery of gold in California in 1849 also contributed to the westward movement, as hordes of opportunists rushed to California to try to get rich. Another incentive to westward settlements was the Homestead Act, passed by Congress in 1862, which granted that an American citizen could use up to 160 acres of public land, and that if he lived on the land for five years and built a home on it, he could buy the property for ten dollars. By Melville's death, 48 million acres were occupied (Horton and Edwards, 130).

Social Problems and Progress

While the westward movement was positive for many, for others—Indians, Mexicans, and blacks—it caused bitterness. For example, the Cherokees of Georgia were evicted from their land and forced to move west; thousands died on the way on a route that has become known as "the trail of tears." Clashes with Mexicans also took place, as Americans crowded into lands once owned by them.

However, the greatest conflict was over slavery. Although government officials tried many compromises, such as the Compromise of 1850, nothing eased tensions between North and South. Therefore, when abolitionist Abraham Lincoln was elected president in 1860, the South seceded from the Union, and the Civil War raged from 1861 to 1865. After General Lee's surrender at Appomattox, slavery was at an end in the United States.

Melville was deeply concerned over racial issues and the war, as seen in many of his works, especially in *Benito Cereno* (1855), in which Melville examines relationships between black slaves and white owners, and *Battle-Pieces and Other Aspects of the War* (1866), a collection of poems about the Civil War that convey, according to Edmund Wilson, "the patriotic feelings of an anxious middle-aged non-combatant as, day by day, he reads the bulletins from the front" (quoted in Delbanco, 268).

Economic and Material Progress

Business and industry flourished in the nineteenth century. One major New England business was whaling, a thriving industry until 1859, when petroleum was discovered in Pennsylvania. Whale blubber was used for illumination (household lamps, streetlights, lighthouses, locomotive headlights) and lubrication (factory machinery, sewing machines, clocks); whale bristle was made into brushes and brooms; whalebone was used as plastic is today; whale spermaceti was converted into high-quality candles; and whale ambergris was transformed into perfume (Delbanco, 38).

Other industries were also prominent in New England, especially cotton factories. After the Civil War ended in the late 1860s, new industries arose throughout the country: steel, railroads, meat-packing, and petroleum (Horton and Edwards, 142–144). As people pushed westward and began farming larger plots of land, machinery improved; reapers, binders, and threshers were invented. Other scientific devices, such as fertilizers and insecticides, helped increase crop production (Blair, et al., 148). Communication methods also became better, as the telegraph and telephone came into use.

A major result of the industrial revolution was the rise of the cities on the eastern seaboard. In particular, New York City grew from a hundred thousand people in 1819 to over 3 million when Melville died in 1891. Immigrants flocked to the city, making housing expensive and hard to get. Commercial buildings were constructed close together and towered high into the skies, as Melville describes the law office building in "Bartleby." By the time Melville wrote *Billy Budd* in the late 1880s, New York City was much like the present-day metropolis, "a place of skyscrapers and cavernous streets, electrified, increasingly international, crisscrossed by mechanized trains and trolleys with

WHALING, A MAJOR BUSINESS OF NEW ENGLAND UNTIL 1859 WHEN PETROLEUM WAS DISCOVERED IN PENNSYLVANIA, WAS AN EXCITING BUT EXTREMELY DANGEROUS BIG GAME HUNT. WHALES WOULD SOMETIMES ATTACK AND DESTROY SMALL WHALEBOATS, PITCHING THE MEN IN THEM INTO THE OPEN OCEAN.

the beginnings of a subway system below, linked to the neighboring municipality of Brooklyn by a traffic-laden suspension bridge" (Delbanco, 315).

The Importance of Evolutionary Thought

Scientific advances affected the religious thought of the nineteenth century. Of greatest importance was Charles Darwin's work on the theory of evolution. Beginning with *Origin of Species* in 1859, Darwin showed that humans developed slowly from simpler forms of life, thus challenging the Christian belief in the unique creation of mankind. As a result, many people, including Melville, began to lose faith in God and in the dignity and worth of humans. Melville's 1876 poem, *Clarel*, examines Christian doctrines in light of these scientific advances.

Literary Progress

During the first half of the nineteenth century, American literature began to flourish. About one hundred novels were published by American authors in the 1820s; in the 1830s, Americans produced three hundred; but by the 1840s, when Melville published his first novels, the number "leapt toward a thousand" (Delbanco, 76).

Not only were more literary pieces produced, they also began to be recognized as serious works of art. When Melville was writing and publishing his famous novels from 1845 to 1857, other American writers, who formed the American Renaissance, were also recognized as important: Washington Irving, James Fenimore Cooper, Edgar Allan Poe, Ralph Waldo Emerson, Henry David Thoreau, Nathaniel Hawthorne, and Walt Whitman. Another writer, Harriet Beecher Stowe, became famous overnight with the publication of *Uncle Tom's Cabin* in 1851.

After the Civil War, new writers emerged, including Mark Twain, William Dean Howells, Henry James, and Emily Dickinson. By the end of the century, American literature was internationally recognized.

MELVILLE'S FIRST BOOK, *TYPEE*, PUBLISHED IN 1846, MADE THE AUTHOR FAMOUS AS THE "MAN WHO LIVED AMONG THE CANNIBALS." THE TITLE PAGE AND FRONTISPIECE OF THE FIRST EDITION IMMEDIATELY ESTABLISH THE BOOK AS A TRAVEL ADVENTURE TALE TAKING PLACE IN THE REMOTE MARQUESAS ISLANDS.

Chapter 3

Typee

YEARS BEFORE MELVILLE WROTE *Moby Dick*, he was known as the "man who lived among the cannibals." The "scandalous, enthralling, and yes, titillating story" (Sullivan, xiii) of the time he lived with the South Sea cannibals was told in his first novel, *Typee: A Peep at Polynesian Life*, published in 1846.

Plot

To escape the confinement and tyranny on the whaling ship, sailor Tommo, the narrator and protagonist, decides to desert the *Dolly* with his companion Toby when the ship is harbored on the Marquesan island of Nukuheva. They hope to find protection with the friendly Happars while avoiding the cannibalistic Typees. However, after struggling across rugged mountains and becoming lost, the men stagger into the valley of the dreaded Typees. To their delight, the Typees are hospitable people and their way of life seems idyllic. Tommo, who has an injured leg, is served by a handsome young man, Kory-Kory, and is loved by the beautiful island girl Fayaway. When Toby disappears after leaving to get help for his friend, Tommo fears that he has been eaten by the cannibals. At the same time he recognizes that the Typees are holding him captive. Fearful of being tattooed or eaten, Tommo makes a daring escape when an Australian whaler anchors nearby. Years later, he finds out that Toby had also escaped.

Themes and Issues

Melville's primary theme is the contrast between civilized and primitive societies. It is subdivided into three topics: the evils of civilization, the idyllic qualities of primitive societies, and the shortcomings of primitive societies. The first two topics are found throughout the book as Melville compares corrupt nineteenth-century Europeans and Americans to happy, pleasure-seeking Polynesians.

The Evils of Civilization

From the very beginning, Melville proclaims the evils of civilization as he describes the "privations and hardships" (3) of life on a whaler: the sick were "inhumanly neglected"; food was "scanty"; cruises were "unreasonably protracted"; and the captain was "arbitrary and violent in the extreme" (21). Under these tyrannical conditions, Tommo feels justified in breaking his contract and deserting the ship.

Besides mistreating its own members, civilized society also imposes great evils upon primitive peoples through commerce and contact. Tommo, deeply saddened as he watches the sailors' "riot and debauchery" (15) when the lovely Marquesan girls board their ship, "weeps over the ruin thus remorselessly inflicted upon them by their European civilizers" and laments the "contaminating contact with the white man" (15). Even worse than the sailors are the colonizers who destroy the natives and fall into moral decay. Tommo, sickened by the French warship that has anchored at the island, sarcastically declares: "Four heavy, double-banked frigates and three corvettes to frighten a parcel of naked heathen into subjection! Sixty-eight pounders to demolish huts of cocoa-nut boughs, and Congreve rockets to set on fire a few canoe sheds!" (16) Conquerors are strongly condemned as "vipers whose sting is destined to poison all their joys" (26) as "they burn, slaughter, and destroy" (27) the natives.

However, Melville reserves his greatest criticism for the Christian missionaries who impose their religion on the natives while reducing them to slavelike or even subhuman positions. He tells of a missionary's wife who rode daily in her cart pulled by two of her native converts whom she used as draught horses (196–197). Over and over again he blasts the Christian missionaries who bring "disease, vice, and premature death" (195) to the heathens.

The Idyllic Qualities of Primitive Societies

Contrasted to this negative view of civilization is the idyllic picture of the primitive, innocent Polynesians who live on an Edenlike island in "mirth, fun, and high good humor" (126) because "the penalty of the Fall presses very lightly upon the valley of Typee" (195). Throughout, they are pictured as noble savages, Jean-Jacques Rousseau's view of mankind in which humans who live close to nature in primitive societies are intrinsically good but become corrupted by civilization. As noble savages, the Marquesans do not work but instead spend their days swimming, riding boats, taking walks, visiting, napping, and eating fruit from the abundant fruit trees. They have "no cares, griefs, troubles or vexations" (126). Since they do not own personal property, they have no debts, thefts, or jealousies. Melville sums it up with one word: "no Money! That 'root of all evil' was not to be found in the valley" (126). Thus, the Typee valley, where handsome Kory-Kory waits on him and lovely Fayaway is his constant companion, seems to be paradise.

The Shortcomings of Primitive Societies

But however much he praises the Polynesians and mourns their loss of innocence as they come in contact with Europeans, Melville finds major deficiencies in their society, recognizing "the horror that exists not far beneath the placid surface" (Miller, 33). Therefore, Tommo takes the first chance he gets to escape.

As many critics have pointed out, the most depraved aspect of Polynesian culture is cannibalism (Breitwieser, 405; Butterfield, 22; Ivison, 126; Miller, 32–34), an evil practiced by the savages long before they had any contact with whites. The threat of cannibalism is woven throughout the book. Even before he sets foot on the island, Tommo relates that "the word Typee . . . signifies a lover of human flesh." The fear of being eaten reaches its climax when Tommo discovers three human heads—two islanders and one white man's. From then on, he agonizes over how he can escape, and when the opportunity arises, he becomes desperately aggressive towards those islanders who try to restrain him.

Another native practice Tommo finds repulsive, tattooing, provides the second reason he desires to escape. He realizes that if he is forcibly tattooed, he is forever marked as a member of the Typees and can never return home because he will not be accepted into Western society.

Although Tommo's greatest fears are being eaten or tattooed, there are three other compelling reasons that he wants to escape and return to civilization, where he finds greater happiness. First, as a thinking man, Tommo is bored because of the mental stupor found on the Polynesian island where life "is little else than an often interrupted and luxurious nap" (152). A man raised in a Western culture, filled with intellectual striving, could never be happy living in a land devoted to merely sensual, animal-like pleasure, "nearly devoid of any life of the mind or of the spirit" (Miller, 31).

Another fault Tommo finds with the Typees is that they do not see people as individual beings. With no selfhood, there is no sense of direction and no meaning for life. Thus, as Mitchell Breitwieser points out, Tommo leaves, preferring "a balked and dominated self to no self at all" (410).

The Polynesian society lacks one other element Westerners like Tommo consider essential for happiness: freedom. Although Tommo deserts the *Dolly* in quest of freedom, he enters into another kind of captivity in the Typee Valley. Physically, Tommo is restrained, for the savages never allow him to travel around the island by himself, and they aggressively hold him back as he tries to get on board the ship which will return him to civilization. Emotionally, they try to bind him to them forever, urging him to get tattooed and be recognized as a Typee.

Thus Melville shows that the Typees are appealing when he compares them to corrupted Western culture, but they are repulsive when they threaten his body, his mind, and his free, individual self.

Analysis

Structure

Typee is a hybrid book that belongs in two genres. It is both an informative travel narrative and an entertaining novel. Therefore, Melville, who claims his book is a true account of his adventures, includes much nonfiction— describing customs, scenery, and historical events that do not add to the plot or develop characters—but he also fills the book with suspenseful episodes.

Although some critics feel the plot is obscured by the "long and tiresome essays on anthropology, sociology, and history of the Marquesas" (Hall, 51), the book does have a form; it is divided into three main sections. The first section, the story of Tommo and Toby's flight from civilization, describes the horrific conditions on board the *Dolly*, the paradisiacal qualities of Polynesian society, and Tommo and Toby's daring escape over the mountains. The second section, and the longest, is the story of Tommo's life in the exotic world of the Typees: Tommo and Toby's entry into the Typee valley, the disappearance and feared cannibalistic eating of Toby, a series of descriptions of the Typees and their lives, Marnoo's visit, and Tommo's fears that the natives are fattening him to eat him. The third section is the story of Tommo's daring getaway from the island. The book concludes with a sequel that relates Toby's escape. Melville's blend of fact and fiction make this book both a travel narrative and a novel.

Point of View

Everything is told by Tommo, who appears to be almost identical to Melville. He fluctuates between two different times in his life. Sometimes he writes as a young, romantic adventurer who is experiencing the events as they are told. Other times, he is an older, wiser, more cynical writer who remembers the events that took place four years earlier. Whatever his age, Tommo interjects humor and irony throughout his tale, and he speaks in a simple, direct language.

Tommo is an outsider who never commits himself to one society. Therefore, although he blasts civilization for destroying the savages of Polynesia, he wants to return to civilized land, and although he praises the innocence and goodness of the Typees, he fears they will eat him or brand him with a tattoo.

Characters

Tommo, the narrator and central figure, is a young adventurous romantic who signs on a whaler to see the world. When he fails to find happiness on the oppressive ship, he looks for it in the heathen land of the Polynesians. But here, too, he cannot find lasting bliss and escapes back to civilization. Tommo is a thinking man who harshly criticizes the actions of civilized people that bring harm to the native Polynesians. He is also a fun-loving man with a great sense of humor. Tommo laces his tale with hilarious anecdotes, such as his story of the Polynesian queen who bared her "own sweet form" to show the shocked Frenchmen her tattoos. (8)

Tommo's fellow adventurer, Toby, is a brave but quiet man who never reveals his thoughts. Very practical and cynical, he provides a contrast to the romantic Tommo. The Polynesians are seen as noble savages in several characters. Tommo's love—the beautiful, sensuous, innocent Fayaway—is the essence of noble savage womanhood. It is her body, not her inner character, that Tommo dwells on: her lovely olive skin, enchanting blue eyes, luxurious brown hair, and gorgeous figure. Another noble savage is Tommo's bodyguard and male nurse, Kory-Kory, who thoughtfully and kindly attends to Tommo's needs. Marnoo, the "taboo" man who is free to travel from tribe to tribe, is a superior noble savage. Heroic and handsome, Tommo calls him a "Polynesian Apollo" (135). Finally, the chief of the Typees, Mehevi, is the supreme example of "Nature's noblemen" (78). Noble and dignified, he is also very generous, feeding Tommo with the best foods, agreeing to let Fayaway join him in a canoe, granting him permission to go to the ocean, and allowing him to remain tattooless. Yet Tommo seems to fear this powerful man.

Imagery and Motifs
The Garden of Eden
The most common imagery in *Typee* relates to the Garden of Eden, which Melville uses ironically to show both the noble and depraved aspects of the island. Therefore, although Tommo describes the island as a type of paradise, he and Toby almost immediately discover that it is not. They become trapped by thick, impenetrable reeds; risk their lives on the rugged mountains; almost starve because there is nothing to eat; and drink water that tastes like ash (53). There even seems to be a serpent lurking in this paradise, for Tommo is sick after his leg is bitten by "some venomous reptile" (48). Other things are not as

perfect as they appear: what should be "delicious fruit" (67) is decayed, and the Adam-and-Eve-like lovers, who are "slender and graceful, and completely naked, with the exception of a slight girdle of bark" (68), soon become "wily" (69). This view of the Garden of Eden as a flawed place continues throughout the book, culminating in Tommo's discovery that his Edenlike hosts are, indeed, cannibals.

Tommo's Leg Injury

Some people see Tommo's infected leg as symbolic of his attitudes towards the Typees. When he is afraid that he and Toby may stumble into the valley of the cannibals, Tommo injures his leg, becoming lame. It is only after he is gently cared for by Kory-Kory that Tommo relaxes, and as a result, his leg gets better. However, when he discovers that his hosts are truly cannibals and when they express a desire to tattoo him, his leg acts up again. Therefore, the physical injury mirrors Tommo's mental anguish.

Literary Reception of Novel

Typee was "a famous book, much talked about, even notorious" (Parker, 1:453). Reviewers praised the book for its "freshness and originality," "animation and vivacity," and "easy, gossiping style." Nathaniel Hawthorne, who had not yet met Melville, admired the "lightly but vigorously written" book, while Walt Whitman gushed that it is "unsurpassed" as a book to "pore dreamily over of a summer day."

In spite of the praise, some people faulted the book, which was published as a real-life experience, for its lack of truthfulness. The London *Times* questioned whether a common seaman could have written so excellent a book, while others wondered how much of the book was autobiography and how much "monstrous exaggeration." However, Melville's claim that he wrote the "unvarnished truth" (xx) was supported by Toby Green, who wrote, in the summer of 1846, that he was "happy to testify to the entire accuracy of the work" (Leyda, 1:220). Nevertheless, readers continued to doubt the book's authenticity.

Attacks also came from the religious press, which did not like Melville's treatment of missionaries. The *Christian Parlor Magazine* condemned Melville for his "flagrant outrages" against missionary work, while the *American Review* blasted his remarks on the missionaries as "prejudiced and unfounded." Also faulted as loose and immoral because of its casual treatment of sex, critics condemned *Typee* as "voluptuous" and "perverse."

But neither the questions of truthfulness, the hostility of the religious press, nor the moral outrage stopped the acclamations of the "multitude [which went] crazy with delight" (Arvin, 4).

In spite of all the clamor over the book, *Typee* was not a bestseller, with only 4,104 copies sold by December 1847, and the publishers told Melville they did not expect there to "be any great gain[s]" in profits (Parker, 1:575).

Today the novel is readily available from a number of publishers, it is frequently analyzed in professional journals, and it is fairly popular with readers. As Robert Sullivan says, those who read Melville's first book are in for a treat because *Typee* contains Melville's "effortless style, the lush and poemlike descriptions, the Joycean humor (why is everyone always so *serious* about Melville?). On top of all that, it's a great read, a legitimate adventure. Are our wounded hero's newfound pagan friends feeding him or fattening him, and how exactly will he escape?" (xiii).

THIS WOOD ENGRAVING, MADE IN THE LATE NINETEENTH CENTURY, IS THE ONLY KNOWN PICTURE OF MOBY DICK DRAWN DURING HERMAN MELVILLE'S LIFETIME. IT IS LABELED "PEHE NU-E," WHICH APPEARS TO BE A VARIATION OF "PEHEE-NUEE-NUEE," AN ERROMANGOAN WORD FOR "WHALE" THAT IS LISTED IN MELVILLE'S INTRODUCTORY SECTION OF MOBY DICK CALLED "ETYMOLOGY."

Chapter 4

Moby Dick

MOBY DICK, PUBLISHED in 1851, is a rich work of art with an exciting plot, a multitude of facts, a wealth of philosophical statements, and a huge number of comparisons and symbols. So complex is it that experts have had trouble placing it in a literary genre, calling it a prose epic, a prose allegory, an extended prose poem, a symbolic romance, a romance of the sea, a metaphysical novel, a psychological novel, a saga of the whale, and a tale of tragic adventure. But, as critic John D. Reeves points out, "no one classification says enough—a shortfall that testifies to the vast complexity of *Moby Dick*" (5). He, like many others, therefore, simply calls this vast work a novel.

Plot

Ishmael, the narrator of the story, is a Manhattan man who desires to go to sea as an ordinary sailor. Therefore, he travels to the seaport town of New Bedford and rents a room at the Spouter-Inn, sharing his lodging with a tattooed pagan harpooner named Queequeg. Although at first frightened, Ishmael soon admires the South Sea Islander, and they become best friends. They head for Nantucket to find a whaling ship and sign on to the *Pequod*. Before leaving, they receive portentous warnings about sailing with Captain Ahab, and Ishmael sees mysterious dark figures boarding the *Pequod*.

After the *Pequod* has been sailing for days, Ahab, an imposing man with an artificial leg made of whale bone, finally appears. Later, the captain nails a gold coin to the ship's mast, offering to reward it to the first man to sight the White Whale, Moby Dick. Excitedly, the crew pledges to pursue this whale. The enigmatic dark figures, Ahab's secret crew, appear when the first whale is sighted. After a whale is killed, the process of stripping the blubber and extracting its oil begins.

When the *Pequod* meets other ships, Ahab asks if they have seen Moby Dick. On the epidemic-infested *Jeroboam*, which has recently lost one of its men to the White Whale, a deranged sailor warns Ahab of his impending death if he pursues Moby Dick. On another, the hospitable *Samuel Enderby*, the captain who lost an arm to the White Whale tells Ahab not to look for the dangerous animal. But Ahab relentlessly keeps chasing Moby Dick. Queequeg becomes violently ill and asks the carpenter to make him a coffin in the shape of a canoe. When he suddenly gets well, his coffin is made into a lifebuoy.

The hunt for Moby Dick becomes more intense when the *Pequod* enters the Pacific Ocean. Nothing will stop Ahab from his mad pursuit of the leviathan—not the violent typhoon which rips the sails and destroys the compass; not the captain of the *Rachel*, who begs Ahab to help him look for his lost young son who had been in a whaleboat towed by Moby Dick; not the skeleton ship, the *Delight*, which is burying a man killed by the White Whale.

When Ahab spots Moby Dick, a forceful three-day battle occurs. The first two days, Moby Dick, although harpooned, continually attacks the boats, destroying them and killing Ahab's harpooner, Fedallah. The third day, the furious whale rams his head into the *Pequod*, making a huge hole. Desperately, Ahab plunges a harpoon into Moby Dick, but the attached rope catches his neck and yanks him into the ocean as the *Pequod* sinks. Ishmael, the only survivor, floats on Queequeg's coffin/lifebuoy until he is rescued by the *Rachel*.

IN JOHN HUSTON'S MAJESTIC 1956 FILM OF *MOBY DICK*, FRIEDRICH
VON LEDEBUR IS MADE UP FOR HIS ROLE OF THE TATTOOED QUEEQUEG.
THE HARPOON HEAD PROTRUDES OVER HIS RIGHT SHOULDER, SHOWING
HIS OCCUPATION. THE FILM STARRED GREGORY PECK AS CAPTAIN AHAB.

Themes and Issues

Ishmael declares: "To produce a mighty book, you must choose a mighty theme. No great and enduring volume can ever be written on the flea" (Chapter 104; 407). In *Moby Dick*, Melville created a work that is rich with mighty themes.

The Impossibility of Understanding the Universe

Ishmael searches for the truth about life by going to sea, explaining that "in landlessness alone resides the highest truth, shoreless, indefinite as God" (95). He learns that "life—the cosmos and everything in it taken as a microcosm—confronts man as a compelling but insoluble mystery" (Hayford, 659). There are two primary ways Ishmael reveals this truth. First, he shows that human knowledge is always limited no matter how much information is used. This is seen in his attempt to understand the whale, for even though he uses nearly every possible system of knowledge—art, literature, history, folklore, taxonomy, and phrenology—his understanding is incomplete; the whale, a symbol of the universe, is unknowable. Second, he explains that humans can see only the surfaces, not the hidden depths, of things, such as the fathomless ocean, making full knowledge impossible. The "ambiguity, the inconstancy, the incongruity of the natural world" (Hardwick, 87) cannot be understood.

Multiplicity of Meanings in the Universe

Repeatedly, Ishmael discusses the multiplicity of meanings found in the ocean, whales, and the whaling industry. For example, he shows that since the color "white" can be seen in a number of valid ways (Chapter 42), the albino whale should also be viewed in a multitude of ways. Melville explores this theme again as he compares the vision of the whale with the eyesight of humans, explaining that mankind's eyes, which face frontward, can only focus on

AMERICAN ARTIST ROCKWELL KENT CREATED HUNDREDS OF STRIKING
ILLUSTRATIONS FOR A 1930 LANDMARK EDITION OF MELVILLE'S CLASSIC
MOBY DICK. IN CHAPTER 134, "THE CHASE—SECOND DAY," MOBY
DICK RACES THROUGH THE WATERS AND ATTACKS THE WHALEBOATS,
DESTROYING AHAB'S BOAT, SNAPPING OFF HIS IVORY LEG, AND CAUSING
FEDALLAH'S DEATH.

one thing at a time, whereas whales' eyes, which are on opposite sides of their heads, force them to see two images at once. As a result, people are mistakenly prone to regard things in only one way while whales accurately see multiple meanings (Chapter 74).

Dangers in the Universe

Although the universe is neither benevolent nor malevolent, it is an unsafe place. Alfred Kazin lists episode after episode in which the horror of nature is seen: "You see it in the scene of the whale running through the herd with a cutting spade in his body, cutting down his own; in the sharks eating at their own entrails and voiding from them in the same convulsion; in the terrible picture of Pip the cabin boy jumping out of the boat in fright and left on the Pacific to go crazy; in Tashtego falling into the 'honey head' of the whale; in the ropes that suddenly whir up from the spindles and carry you off; in the final awesome picture of the whale butting its head against the *Pequod*" (57–58). Although some humans try to control dangerous elements in the universe through physical attacks or intellectual cunning, no person can master nature.

Different Points of View

Throughout the novel, Melville shows that there are different points of view for just about everything. For example, various men looking at the same coin see entirely different things (Chapter 99), and the nine ship meetings present dissimilar views of Moby Dick. Ishmael, open to different perspectives, encourages readers to also be open-minded.

Although he refuses to state that a particular point of view is right, Ishmael is clear that not all opinions are equally valid, as seen in his condemnation of the three mates who each have a narrow-minded view of life. He calls all "morally enfeebled"—dutiful Starbuck because of "incompetence of mere unaided virtue or right-mindedness," happy-go-lucky Stubb by his "invulnerable jollity of indifference and recklessness," and self-interested Flask for his "pervading mediocrity" (167).

Isolation

Like many authors of his time, Melville believed that isolation, whether caused by outside forces or self-inflicted, is bad. The horror of loneliness, of being cut off from others, is shown vividly through little Pip, who was abandoned in the ocean after jumping from the whaleboat and goes crazy. The evils of self-imposed isolation are shown through Ahab, who cuts himself off from all others, even refusing to help his fellow Nantucketer, the grieving captain of the *Rachel*, search for his missing son. Melville shows that those like Pip who are forced into solitude are to be pitied, while those like Ahab who keep themselves apart from others create grief for themselves and suffering for others.

Friendship

Opposed to Ahab's self-centered isolation is the camaraderie of Ishmael and Queequeg. Ishmael says that becoming "bosom friends" with Queequeg saves his soul: "I felt a melting in me. No more my splintered heart and maddened hand were turned against the wolfish world. This soothing savage had redeemed it" (46, 45). Forming this friendship is a radical gesture because it crosses cultural and religious barriers as the educated, white, Christian American comes to respect and love a tattooed, dark-skinned pagan. Melville shows their brotherhood vividly when Ishmael, tethered to the monkey-rope on board the ship, endangers his life to protect Queequeg from falling into the shark-infested ocean.

Friendship is also found on the *Pequod* as the mates, harpooners, and crew help one another, participate in common duties, and face common dangers. Caring for one another in spite of different cultures and opposing viewpoints is very important to Ishmael, because it makes him happy. A euphoric Ishmael, while squeezing spermaceti, wants to squeeze everyone's hands until everyone is transformed "into the very milk and sperm of kindness" (Chapter 94; 373).

Analysis
Point of View
The novel is told from the point of view of Ishmael, a seaman who has survived a shipwreck and is writing about it. He tells two different stories: first, the tale of the disaster of the *Pequod*, which happened in the past when he was a younger man; second, his reflections of the event, which occur in the present.

Throughout most of the story, the narrator is a thoughtful observer or participant. But sometimes he moves out of the way and speaks from an omniscient point of view, such as when he relates the personal reflections of Ahab, Starbuck, Stubb, and Flask; or when he tells incidents that occur in Ahab's quarters. He employs two unusual forms in his novel: the drama form, observed in such scenes as the one on the forecastle after the men have sworn to aid Ahab pursue the White Whale (Chapter 40); and the sermon form, both Father Mapple's chapel sermon and Fleece's words to the sharks.

The storyteller makes readers active participants in the book by directly addressing them in such lines as "Call me Ishmael" (1). Sometimes he treats readers as intimate friends and carries on conversations with them: "But thou sayest, methinks this white-lead chapter about whiteness is but a white flag hung out from a craven soul; thou surrenderest to a hypo, Ishmael" (174); he confidentially tells them secrets: "Whisper it not, and I will tell" how the mystic albatross has been caught (170); and he makes

MOBY DICK
BY
HERMAN MELVILLE

CAPTAIN AHAB, RECOGNIZABLE BY HIS IVORY LEG, HAS LONG
FASCINATED READERS OF *MOBY DICK*. VERY FEW COPIES OF THE NOVEL
SOLD IN THE FORTY YEARS BETWEEN ITS PUBLICATION IN 1851 AND
MELVILLE'S DEATH IN 1891, BUT SINCE THE MELVILLE REVIVAL IN THE
1920s, THE BOOK HAS BEEN REGARDED AS MELVILLE'S MASTERPIECE
AND IS POPULAR WITH READERS, SCHOLARS, FILMMAKERS, AND WRITERS.

them feel as if they are on the ship with him: "But a day or two after, you look about you, and prick your ears in this self-same ship; and were it not for the tell-tale boats and try-works, you would all but swear you trod some silent merchant vessel" (382).

Often Ishmael acts as a teacher to his readers by sharing information: "I shall ere long paint to you as well as one can without canvas, something like the true form of the whale as he actually appears to the eye of the whaleman" (236); enlightening readers: "But what is a *Gam*? You might wear out your index-finger running up and down the columns of dictionaries, and never find the word. . . . With that view, let me learnedly define it"; (216) and teaching truths about life: "Give not thyself up, then, to fire, lest it invert thee, deaden thee; as for the time it did me" (380).

By using various forms and forming an intimate relationship with readers, Melville's narrator tells a gripping, complex story.

Style
Rhetoric

Melville's narrator adopts several types of rhetoric to tell his story: expository, colloquial, and poetic. Sometimes he straightforwardly tells of events or gives definitions in expository style. Other times he employs colloquial language, such as when Fleece, the black cook, talks to the sharks: "Your woraciousness, fellow-critters, I don't blame ye so much for; dat is natur, and can't be helped; but to gobern dat wicked natur, dat is de pint" (266). Much of the time, Melville adopts a poetic style of language. Even a cursory glance at the book reveals his great use of poetic devices. For instance, in one paragraph, he includes alliteration (repetition of initial sounds): "continual command," "drenched and dangerous deck," "tempestuous times." "Captain and crew," "squall of sleet or snow," and "burstingly broke over its bows"; rhyme (repetition of end sounds): "madness and gladness"; and parallel words and clauses: "above and aloft, "sleet or snow," "still in silence the men swung in the bowlines; still wordless Ahab stood up to the blast" (211).

Figurative Language

A predominant feature of Melville's art is his use of figurative language, especially similes. For example, he compares the gluttonous sharks feasting on the dead whale to Old Testament Israelites "thirstily drinking . . . at the new bursting fountains that poured from the smitten rock" (291). He says a cavity in the Sperm Whale's head "may be regarded as the great Heidelburgh Tun" (304). He asserts that "like Shadrach, Meshach, and Abednego" (Daniel 3:19–27), the whale's "spermaceti, oil, and bone pass unscathed through the fire" (381). He says that the ship with all its cargo on deck is top-heavy "as a dinnerless student with all Aristotle in his head" (424).

He also uses metaphors. Melville spends an entire chapter referring to the Sperm Whale's head as "the Sphynx" (Chapter 70) and another calling it "the praire" (Chapter 79). The whale's brain becomes "the nut" (Chapter 80), while the thin skin covering his male organ is dried and made into a "cassock" (Chapter 95).

Melville gleans his comparisons from three main sources: the Bible, drawing from the books of Genesis, Exodus, Kings, Daniel, Job, Jonah, the gospels, St. Paul's epistles, and Revelation; historical figures, including Greek thinkers, Roman statesmen, military leaders, artists, writers, kings, and mythological gods; and the American frontier, referring to Native Americans, frontier heroes, and western landscapes and animals.

The figurative language not only adds a poetic quality to the novel, but it also helps readers conceptualize Melville's characters, happenings, and ideas.

Structure

Moby Dick is an adventure story told in two realms: it is a tale of physical conquest and defeat, as well as a meditative journey of a reflective, thoughtful mind.

The main story line consists of the whaling voyage and shipwreck of the *Pequod* as Captain Ahab embarks on his mission to destroy the White Whale. It is an exciting tale of physical adventure that "takes place in a world of athletic heroism, . . . [and] is filled with boasting talk, odd characters, rough deeds, alarums, accidents, mysteries, and narrow escapes" (Parke, 66).

But Melville does not construct his book as a straightforward story with one plot. Instead, much of the novel consists of digressions on the natural world, whales, and the whaling industry. Skillfully, he is able to "describe the appearance, the concrete matter-of-factness, and the utility of each one of these natural objects, implements, and tools with the fidelity of a scientist, and while doing this, explore it as a conceivable repository of some aspect of the human drama; then, by an imaginative tour de force, deliver a vital essence, some humorous or profound idea, coalescing with its embodiment" (Murray, 26). Ishmael's many non-narrative chapters add a richness to this novel rarely seen in works of literature.

The Non-Narrative Chapters

The digressive chapters, linked by themes or images, are included for a variety of reasons—to impart knowledge, add humor, and examine truths about man, nature, life, and the universe.

The Opening: "Etymology"; "Etymology"; "Extracts"; "Extracts"

Before he begins chapter 1, Melville includes many pages of information about whales to set the tone, establish the subject, and introduce the themes of the novel. Opening sarcastically in "Etymology," Melville shows the limited knowledge of an educator who simplistically seeks to describe unknowable whales by using "old lexicons and grammars" (xl). Usher, an assistant schoolmaster, is poor and weak financially, emotionally, physically, and intellectually. Melville calls him "threadbare in coat, heart, body, and brain" (xl).

Opposed to Usher is the Sub-Sub-Librarian of the first "Extracts" section, a man little valued by the world but much admired by Melville because he tries to look at whales from all points of view by combing a multitude of books to find allusions to these mighty creatures. The extracts give "a glancing bird's eye view of what has been promiscuously said, thought, fancied, and sung of Leviathan, by many nations and generations, including our own" (xlii).

In the second "Extracts" section, Melville provides a series of quotes about whales to show them in a variety of ways. A whale is seen as both a "great" creation of God that "play[s]" in the ocean (xliii) and also a "piercing," "crooked serpent" (xliii) "that maketh the seas to seethe like boiling pan" (xliv). This creature of "monstrous bulk" (xliv) is a prized animal because it yields an "incredible quantity of oil" (xliv), but it is also a dreaded monster because it "threatens ruin with his ponderous tail" (xliv), can destroy "all other things, whether beast or vessel" (xliv) with its "gaping jaws" (xlv), and fights fiercely for its life, destroying men and ships so that "out of the crew of Whaling vessels (American) few ever return in the ships on board of which they departed" (li). This paradoxical, unknowable "King of the boundless sea" (lii), who is seen as both majestic and evil, playful and powerful, valuable and terrifying, is thus introduced as the subject of Melville's book.

Chapters 32 and 35: "Cetology"; "The Mast-Head"
Looking at the difficulty of understanding the cosmos,
Ishmael first shares information about the science of whales
(cetology), insisting that information concerning the
leviathans is incomplete and unfinished. Relating this to
humans' knowledge of the universe, he implies that aspects
of life are also vague and cannot be totally understood.

He also describes the masthead, the place perched high
above the deck where sailors stand on two thin bars scan-
ning the horizon for whales, telling how easy it is for a
philosophic man to forget his obligation to watch for
whales and instead daydream. Comparing this meditative
man to a person who can never understand reality because
he is looking for an ideal, he concludes that idealists may
"drop through that transparent air into the summer sea,
no more to rise for ever" (141).

*Chapters 41 and 42: "Moby Dick"; "The Whiteness of
the Whale"*
Both chapters examine reasons for people's terror of Moby
Dick and develop Melville's theme of the multiplicity of
meanings in the universe. Ishmael relates that the White
Whale is feared because of "wild rumors" that he is
"ubiquitous," physically a "monster . . . with unwonted
power," filled with "ferocity," and the manifestation of
"intangible malignity" (160, 162–164). These views of
Moby Dick are, obviously, limited visions of this great
beast.

Ishmael next realistically examines a valid reason for
fear: Moby Dick's white color. He finds that *whiteness* can
symbolize a variety of things, both good and evil: not only
virtue, nobility, holiness, chastity, joy, innocence, religious
purity, and divinity; but also terror, dread, bad omen,
sickness, death, and, worst of all, "the heartless voids and
immensities of the universe" (175). People, he concludes,
fear Moby Dick because the albino whale is a symbol of

all these things. Thus, although Moby Dick is not evil, he terrifies Ishmael, who sees that the universe, like the whale, is not a place of order and kindness, but one of immense voids.

Chapter 47: "The Mat-Maker"
Both a plot and a digressive chapter, "The Mat-Maker" discusses the relationship between mat-making and life, showing that humans are not totally free but also are dependent on chance and necessity.

Chapters 55–57: "Of the Monstrous Pictures of Whales"; "Of the Less Erroneous Pictures of Whales and The True Pictures of Whaling Scenes"; "Of Whales in Paint; In Teeth; In Wood; In Sheet-Iron; In Stone; In Mountains; In Stars"
As Ishmael examines pictures of whales, he advances his idea that fallible humans cannot understand the complex universe. Ishmael relates that land artists, who have never seen whales in their natural state in the ocean, have no true concept of leviathans, although some have a better understanding than others. He feels that only whalemen are able to truly depict them, which they do in their skrimshandering, carvings made from whale bone. Furthermore, whalemen are able to see leviathan likenesses in various parts of the natural world, such as in mountains and star formations.

Chapters 58–60, 62–63, and 66: "Brit"; "Squid"; "The Line"; "The Dart"; "The Crotch"; "The Shark Massacre"
All of these chapters deal with the perils found in life, relating to Melville's theme that dangers abound in the universe.

"Brit" introduces the topic, showing that even things that appear peaceful are surrounded by unperceived dangers for beneath this yellow floating substance that serves as food for whales, the ocean is filled with cannibalistic creatures that are "treacherously hidden beneath the loveliest tints of azure" (248). He compares the dangerous ocean that surrounds "this green, gentle, and most docile earth" to a human soul, where "there lies one insular Tahiti, full of peace and joy, but encompassed by all the horrors of the half known life" (248). This vast cosmos, then, is filled with dangers, causing Ishmael to warn people that if they leave the safety of innocence, they can never again live simplistic lives: "Push not off from that isle, thou canst never return!" (248).

Ishmael elaborates on the perils found in the ocean, discussing first the terrifying giant squid and then manmade dangers, beginning with the whale line, which "carries more of true terror than any other aspect of this dangerous affair [whaling]" (254). He relates it to the threats found in people's lives, declaring that "All men live enveloped in whale-lines. All are born with halters round their necks; but it is only when caught in the swift, sudden turn of death, that mortals realize the silent, subtle, every-present perils of life" (254). The dart, the sharp instrument of death, and the crotch, which houses the harpoons, are two more manmade dangers.

But other perils also confront harpooners. They face exhaustion by straining their muscles in the long chase before throwing their harpoon into the whale. They confront death in the open waters, as they exchange places with the mates in a racing boat towed by a whale. And they face death from the flying harpoons. As is true in life, terrors abound in whaling.

Chapter 66 concludes this section by looking at another terrifying peril of the ocean—sharks. If sailors harpoon these predators as they feed on a newly killed whale, surviving sharks will attack their wounded mates and devour them. Queequeg's observation that "de god wat made shark must be one dam Ingin" (272), helps develop the theme of the universe as a terrifying place with dangers lurking everywhere.

Chapters 67–70: "Cutting In"; "The Blanket"; "The Funeral"; "The Sphynx"
These chapters relate to butchering the whale and provide metaphors for various observations about life. Chapter 67 begins by explaining the dangerous steps taken to remove the blubber. Ishmael then analyzes the nature of a whale's skin, explaining that the seemingly simple subject of "skin" is really a difficult one since he does not know whether a whale's skin is the thin gray covering of its body or if it is the many inches of blubber, once again revealing the theme of the complexity of a universe in which there are no simple answers.

Noting that blubber keeps the whale warm in arctic waters and cool in the tropical oceans, Ishmael meditates on the importance of maintaining individual integrity in a hostile world. He admires the whale with its "rare virtue of a strong individual vitality, and the rare virtue of thick walls, and the rare virtue of interior spaciousness" and admonishes humans to "admire and model thyself after the whale! Do thou, too, remain warm among ice. Do thou, too, live in this world without being of it. Be cool at the equator; keep thy blood fluid at the Pole. Like the great dome of St. Peter's, and like the great whale, retain, O man! in all seasons a temperature of thine own" (277).

After releasing the whale's carcass, Ishmael reflects on the nature of the universe, a hostile world in which even the majestic whale is devoured by voracious sharks and sea birds. He decries the "horrible vultureism of earth! from which not the mightiest whale is free" (278). Ishmael also notes that humans superstitiously fear the unknown, becoming frightened even by the whale's desecrated, ghostlike corpse.

These chapters conclude by looking at the whale's immense head, which resembles a Sphinx, a mythological creature that solves riddles. Although Ahab demands that it tell him the secrets of the universe, it does not, showing the cosmos as complex and its mysteries as unsolvable.

Chapter 72: "The Monkey-Rope"
Both a plot and a digressive chapter, "The Monkey-Rope" describe the rope that ties Ishmael to Queequeg as the latter is cutting into the whale's flesh while standing on its submerged back with sharks prowling the waters beneath it. It symbolizes, first, brotherhood, as Ishmael attempts to keep his friend from harm. Second, it indicates the interrelationship between humans, for Ishmael is aware that his precarious situation "was the precise situation of every mortal that breathes. . . . If your banker breaks, you snap; if your apothecary by mistake sends you poison in your pills, you die" (287). Nevertheless, humans need to be connected to one another to help them avoid the ever-present dangers of life: "That unsounded ocean you gasp in, is Life; those sharks, your foes; those spades, your friends; and what between sharks and spades you are in a sad pickle and peril, poor lad" (289).

*Chapters 74–77, 79–80: "The Sperm Whale's Head—
Contrasted View"; "The Right Whale's Head—
Contrasted View"; "The Battering-Ram"; "The Great
Heidelburgh Tun"; "The Praire"; "The Nut"*
These chapters examine a whale's head, which Melville uses as a major metaphor to illustrate the theme of the multiplicity of meanings found in the universe. Beginning with the whale's eyes, which are widely separated, Ishmael concludes that a whale must see the world in a far different way than humans, who see only what is in front of them. Since the whale can see only one thing at a time, it must see the world in multiple ways, a view Ishmael thinks humans should adopt to better understand the universe.

Looking at the head of the Right Whale, Ishmael continues to develop this theme, stating that "as you come nearer to this great head it begins to assume different aspects, according to your point of view" (299).

By examining various ways the whale uses its head, Ishmael develops additional metaphors proving that the universe must be regarded in a variety of ways. The head is used as a weapon of defense to batter his enemy (Chapter 76); it provides valuable spermaceti for human use (Chapter 77); and it is used for thinking (Chapters 79–80). With its immense forehead, Ishmael concludes that the whale possesses a "high and mighty god-like dignity" that shows "genius" (311). In contrast, most humans have small foreheads, which he equates with small thoughts: "Few are the foreheads which like Shakspeare's [sic] or Melancthon's rise so high, and descend so low" (310). Like the whale's impressive brow that is too complicated to be fully understood ("I but put that brow before you. Read it if you can" [311]), the universe is a complex, inexplicable place.

The examination of the whale's head closes with a look at its small brain cavity, which does not give the full picture of the whale's intelligence since the brain is connected to a huge spinal canal. Ishmael reflects that a noble human, like the majestic whale, will possess a strong backbone, stating, ". . . much of a man's character will be found betokened in his backbone. . . . A thin joist of a spine never yet upheld a full and noble soul" (313).

According to these chapters, the "indomitable" whale (314), a symbol of the vast universe, is filled with complexities which humans can never totally understand.

Chapters 82–84: "The Honor and Glory of Whaling"; "Jonah Historically Regarded"; "Pitchpoling"

These three loosely connected chapters honor great whalemen. First, Ishmael elevates whale-hunting to a noble enterprise by relating stories of whaling heroes—Perseus, who rescued a maiden from a whale; St. George, who battled a dragon that Ishmael insists was a whale; and Hercules, Jonah, and Vishnoo, who made the whale into a holy animal. Next Ishmael examines the veracity of what may be the best-known story of whales: the biblical tale of Jonah. Last, he moves to a present-day hero—a mate like Stubb who can perform a magician-type act with his huge pitchpole, hurling it at the whale while being tossed about on a boat flying through the water.

Chapters 85–90, 92: "The Fountain"; "The Tail"; "The Grand Armada"; "Schools and Schoolmasters"; "Fast-Fish and Loose-Fish"; "Heads or Tails"; "Ambergris"
As Ishmael looks at other aspects of whales, he relates his observations to life. When meditating on the seemingly simple subject of whale spouts, questioning whether they are composed of water or vapor, he shows that life is too complex to fully understand: "My dear sir, in this world it is not so easy to settle these plain things. I have ever found your plain things the knottiest of all" (333–334). He continues this theme as he looks as the whale's tail, trying to see all its complexity: its "vast local power," "most appalling beauty," "exceeding grace," and "great motions" (336–337). But, he recognizes that he is unable to fully describe the tail, just as the complex universe is impossible to understand.

Seeing the Grand Armada, Ishmael's metaphor for a herd of whales, Ishmael realizes that just as the whales are connected to the islands that stretch across the ocean, so all things in the universe are interrelated. "Schools and Schoolmasters" provides additional information about whale herds.

Ishmael talks about "Fast-Fish and Loose-Fish" to criticize manmade laws, noting that human decisions of whale ownership are often unfair, based on human greed.

In "Heads or Tails," Ishmael makes clear that it is impossible to determine a dividing line between the head and the tail of a whale, just as in life it is not feasible to know almost anything with complete confidence.

"Ambergris" concludes this section. Ishmael, after explaining that fragrant ambergris is found inside sick, foul-smelling whales, develops his theme of the ambiguity of nature, since what smells terrible brings forth the best, most expensive perfume.

Chapters 94–98: "A Squeeze of the Hand"; "The Cassock"; "The Try-Works"; "The Lamp"; "Stowing Down and Clearing Up"

Chapters 94–98 deal with the extraction and storing of the whale's oil. Ishmael begins by explaining that the sperm, which had become lumpy as it cooled, needs to be squeezed to change the globules back to a liquid. As he squeezes, a type of euphoria envelops him, and he squeezes the hands of his fellow workers, advising his readers that we need to "squeeze ourselves universally into the very milk and sperm of kindness" (373). Brotherhood and love for others, he realizes, are essential to human beings.

Next, Ishmael tells a coarse joke, describing the whalemen's conversion of the male whale's reproductive organ to a priestlike cassock, worn to protect workers cutting blubber into small pieces called Bible leaves.

The minced blubber is then cooked in the try-pots, rendering it into oil. Watching this process, Ishmael comprehends that the tryworks show that all things of the universe move towards order. He learns a second truth after staring at the fire under the try-pots, an artificial form of light that causes Ishmael to become disoriented, face backwards, and lose sight of the ship's compass. He admonishes readers to be careful about their points of view, for often they are not based on reality: "Look not too long in the face of the fire, O man. . . . Turn not thy back to the compass; . . . believe not the artificial fire. . . . Tomorrow, in the natural sun, the skies will be bright; those who glared like devils in the forking flames, the morn will show in far other, at least gentler, relief; the glorious, golden glad sun, the only true lamp—all others but liars!" (379–380). Ishmael continues his observation that people need true light, truth, to guide them in "The Lamp," noting that "the whaleman, as he seeks the food of light, so he lives in light" (381).

In Chapter 98, Ishmael describes rigorous whaling life, for even as the men are cleaning up from butchering one whale, lookouts are posted to spy another, which will cause the difficult process of extracting oil to begin again. This "man-killing" work is like life: "For hardly have we mortals by long toilings extracted from this world's vast bulk its small but valuable sperm; and then, with weary patience, cleansed ourselves from its defilements, and learned to live here in clean tabernacles of the soul; hardly is this done, when—*There she blows!*—the ghost is spouted up, and away we sail to fight some other world, and go through young life's old routine again" (383).

Chapters 101–105: "The Decanter"; "A Bower in the Arsacides"; "Measurement of the Whale's Skeleton"; "The Fossil Whale"; "Does the Whale's Magnitude Diminish—Will He Perish?"

These five chapters show the immensity of the whaling industry and of whales: a whaling crew requires vast provisions; a whale has a gigantic skeleton, making it difficult to measure; whales seem to live forever. Therefore, whales and whaling are like life—everlasting, vast, complex, and filled with greatness, dangers, and uncertainties.

The Gams

The nine ship meetings, called gams, help give coherence to the plot by developing both the Ahab and the Ishmael aspects of the novel. Each meeting begins with the Captain's question, "Have ye seen the White Whale?" His response to their answers not only shows his obsession with and hostility toward Moby Dick, but also his isolation, for he has no interest in camaraderie or in the welfare of others. The gams also relate to Ishmael, who sees these visits as opportunities for new friendships and the ships as metaphors for life truths. The gams are set up in three sections.

The first two gams, placed close together in chapters 52 and 54, involve ships which seem to have had experience with Moby Dick, although neither communicates its experience to Ahab. The aged *Albatross* should have wisdom, but it fails to exchange even one word with the *Pequod* because the trumpet falls into the sea. To Ishmael, the ship, "bleached like the skeleton of a stranded walrus" (12), foretells death. The men of the *Town-Ho* named for the cry used by whalemen when they first sight a whale (217), definitely know about the White Whale, but they tell their story only to the *Pequod's* crew, not Ahab. Their tale is an exciting one—a malicious, inhumane ship officer named Radney abuses a member of the crew, Steelkilt, who plans to murder the officer, but before he is able to retaliate, Radney is killed by Moby Dick. The men and Ishmael regard the whale as a moral avenging agent that fulfills some sort of divine justice.

Gams 3–7, widely spaced with approximately ten chapters between each, take place in chapters 71, 81, 91, 100, and 115. All of them show attitudes about Moby Dick that are unacceptable to Ahab.

Although the crew of the *Jeroboam* believe in Moby Dick, they do not look upon him realistically but rather through fear and superstition. The ship, named for an evil Old Testament king who helped his people worship false gods, is terrorized by a reprehensible, crazy man who thinks he is the archangel Gabriel. He rages that the mate, Macey, was justly killed by Moby Dick, who Gabriel declares is "the Shaker God incarnated" (284). He further frightens the ignorant crew by declaring that the epidemic on board was brought about by his command. When he warns Ahab that he will find death if he pursues the White Whale, Ahab, unlike the superstitious men of the

Jeroboam, refuses to be intimidated by an irrational madman. To Ishmael, the ship seems aptly named, for Gabriel is much like King Jeroboam, who understands the true nature of things, and the sailors are like Jeroboam's people, allowing themselves to be ruled by a tyrant.

The captains of the next two ships, who are completely ignorant of the White Whale, are shown as dimwitted fools whom neither Ahab nor Ishmael can take seriously. The German *Jungfrau* or *Virgin* represents people who lead innocent lives because of stupidity. The ignorant captain is unable to capture any whales; therefore, his ship, which is in search of oil for the world, has no oil for itself. Last seen, it is chasing a whale that cannot be caught, confusing a Fin-Back for a Sperm Whale. Both Ahab and Ishmael dismiss such uninformed people, realizing that living in ignorance is unacceptable. Ishmael also views this encounter with humor as he, a proud American on a Nantucket ship, shows the stupidity of the unenlightened Germans. The French *Bouton-de-Rose* or *Rose-Bud*, which reeks of decaying whales instead of fragrant roses, is only slightly better. Although it has captured whales, the inexperienced French captain does not know that sick whales contain valuable ambergris and thus allows Stubb to tow away his precious catch. This ship represents inexperience, which realistic Ahab views as another ineffectual attitude toward life. Once again, Ishmael looks at this ship humorously, as he satirizes another non-American ship, showing that the French, who are known for having the best perfume, have no idea how to obtain it.

In contrast to these two foolish captains, Captain Boomer of the *Samuel Enderby*, named for a hospitable English merchant, shows a rational approach to life. After losing an arm to Moby Dick, this captain continues to enjoy life, even joking with the ship's surgeon. He believes that the "noble great whale" (391), an animal that accidentally caused him to lose his arm, should be left alone so no more limbs are lost, an attitude totally rejected by fanatic Ahab. Ishmael, however, appreciates Boomer's advice and revels in his hospitality, finding the *Samuel Enderby* an almost ideal ship.

However, neither Ahab nor Ishmael care for the complacent, fortunate captain of the *Bachelor*, who has heard of the White Whale but childishly declares he "don't believe in him at all" (439). With no intellectual thought and no perception of reality, he is dismissed by Ahab as "a fool" (439), an attitude Ishmael shares.

The last two ships, like the first two, appear close together in chapters 128 and 131. The captains of both whalers believe in Moby Dick, for they have lost many men to him. However, instead of trying to punish him and risk losing more men, both sorrowfully focus on their dead men. The captain of the *Rachel*, named for the mother of the Israelites who weeps for her lost children destroyed by King Herod (Matthew 2:18), has lost six men, including his twelve-year-old son. Although he pleads with Ahab to help him search for his son and crew, Ahab refuses, cutting himself off from all human sympathy. Ishmael, on the other hand, has great pity for this grieving father.

Very soon the *Pequod* meets the "most miserably misnamed" *Delight* (476). Destruction and death are apparent in its splintered whaleboat and the corpse aboard the ship, both destroyed by Moby Dick. Paralyzed into inaction after the encounter, the *Delight* warns Ahab that pursuing the White Whale can lead to annihilation, but Ahab refuses to listen. Ishmael, feeling their anguish and grief, senses that their views are accurate, as the *Pequod* receives a "ghostly baptism" (477) when the *Delight* slips its dead crewman into the ocean.

Through these encounters, Ahab receives warnings and is offered alternative ways of thought and action, but he rejects them all, dooming his crew and himself. Ishmael, however, uses these gams to reflect on people and life.

Characters

Ishmael

The meditative narrator forms the insightful center of the novel. He is like the biblical Ishmael, the outcast son of Abram (who later becomes Abraham) and his servant Hagar who is protected by God. In fact, the name "Ishmael" means "God hears" (Genesis 16:11 and 21:17). Melville's Ishmael is also a protected loner. A thoughtful observer, he is seen both as a young whaler from Manhattan who sailed on the *Pequod* and as an older writer who survived the shipwreck. Young Ishmael is not a major actor in the story of the *Pequod*; in fact, as Alfred Kazin points out, "he is the most insignificant member of the fo'c'sle and will get the smallest share of the take" (54). However, the older Ishmael, according to Walter E. Bezanson, "is the real center of meaning and the defining force of the novel" (644); *Moby Dick* is his story.

Ishmael the writer is a contemplative man who is constantly "absorbing, experiencing, commenting, explaining, but always wondering and never imposing final meaning upon the enigmas that confront him" (C. Cook, 60). He marvels at all he sees—the vast ocean, the mighty whale, and the many types of men. From the first chapter, Ishmael refuses to reduce anything to one simple explanation, even his decision to go to sea: to relieve boredom or depression, to return to the source of life, to earn money, to get exercise, and to satisfy his curiosity.

This thoughtful, intelligent narrator enjoys taking simple, everyday objects and tasks and transforming them into metaphysical speculations. Common whaling tools, aspects of the whaling industry, and physical aspects of whales all become topics for meditations on life in the vast cosmos. His intelligence is further seen in his vast knowledge of Christianity, faraway places, and exotic people.

Kings, philosophers, prophets, mythic heroes, and religious figures all interest him.

Although often serious, the narrator also enjoys laughter and merriment, declaring, "a good laugh is a mighty good thing, and rather too scarce a good thing; the more's the pity" (26). He shows humor with wry statements, such as declaring that whales don't need noses because there are "No roses, no violets, no Cologne-water in the sea" (333). Sometimes he reveals his fun-loving nature by including mocking conclusions. For example, he "proves" his theory that whales spout mist because they think so much, by stating that during a period of deep thought, he noticed an "undulation in the atmosphere over my head," playfully adding that he had just drunk "six cups of hot tea in my thin shingled attic, of an August noon" (335). He uses the same technique when describing Steelkilt, who possesses so great a brain, heart, and soul, "which had made Steelkilt Charlemagne," teasingly concluding, "had he been born son to Charlemagne's father" (221). Occasionally, his jokes are rather crude, such as when he makes a rarely discussed part of the male whale's anatomy a religious symbol (Chapter 95); or when he ponders curing a whale's indigestion "by administering three or four boat loads of Brandreth's pills [laxatives], and then running out of harm's way, as laborers do in blasting rocks" (366). Often he gently laughs at people, relating that young Ishmael, after his first encounter with a whale, rushes to his bunk to make out a will (205), or remarking that Queequeg suddenly recovers from near death because "he had just recalled a little duty ashore, which he was leaving undone; and therefore had changed his mind about dying" (428). For Ishmael, then, humor is a necessity.

It is this contemplative, intelligent, well-read, and humorous narrator who permeates the novel from the first sentence to the last.

Ahab

The captain is the dramatic center of the book. Named after the mighty Old Testament King Ahab who married wicked Jezebel, worshiped the idol Baal, and "did evil in the sight of the Lord more than all that were before him" (I Kings 16:30), Melville's Captain Ahab is also a strong-willed, impressive tyrant who is a "grand, ungodly, god-like man" (71). "Ungodly" Ahab is a type of anti-Job who refuses to acknowledge any power higher than himself. Unlike the biblical Job who humbly recognized God's authority, "Ahab refuses to bend before the whale, who has become both god and devil to him" (Schippe and Stetson, 162), causing Starbuck to accuse him of blasphemy.

Ahab is an imposing figure able to bend the wills of others to his own. A born leader, Ahab understands how to rule a mob, persuading even thoughtful Ishmael to pursue Moby Dick. Intelligent and determined, Ahab also knows how to find the White Whale by studying sea charts and learning the movements of tides and currents. Filled with pride in his abilities, he exclaims, "What I've dared, I've willed; and what I've willed, I'll do!" (149). He is so egotistical that he appears to want to be God.

Although he is convinced that Moby Dick is the incarnation of evil, many critics point out that it is Captain Ahab, instead, who is the "embodiment of that fallen angel or demi-god who in Christendom was variously named Lucifer, Devil, Adversary, Satan" (Murray, 28). In his "overweening pride and arrogance" (R. Cook, 22), much like the pride of Faustus or Prometheus, Ahab forsakes all human ties in his mad hunt.

Like an imposing hero, he dies courageously, trying one last time to harpoon Moby Dick, as "he determines to make [the cosmos] bow to his personal need for revenge" (Parke, 73).

Queequeg

One of the harpooners, Queequeg is from a kingdom in the South Seas. He is seen as a combination of an uncivilized and a civilized human. Although he is an exotic, tattooed savage who sells human heads, Queequeg is also a perfect civilized man—noble, compassionate, fearless, and skillful. Almost immediately, this good man and Ishmael become best friends. His importance as a friend continues to the end of the novel: Ishmael is rescued by floating in the canoe-shaped coffin that Queequeg had built for himself when he thought he was dying.

The Three Mates

Starbuck, Stubb, and Flask, who bow to Ahab's strong will, provide contrasts to the mighty captain.

The first mate, a religious man who relies on his Quaker faith to decide his actions, hunts whales to make a living. Although "uncommonly conscientious," "endued with a deep natural reverence," "careful," and "brave" (101–102), Starbuck is a flawed man who feels duty-bound to obey his captain instead of recognizing his higher duty to the crew. However, he dies honorably, courageously asking God to "stand by me now!" (506).

"Good-humored, easy, and careless" (103) Stubb kills whales for excitement. Always found with a pipe in his mouth, the jolly second mate enjoys life. He faces death in the same jocular manner he lived his life, declaring, "I grin at thee, thou grinning whale!" (506).

Mediocre Flask feels no "reverence for the many marvels" of whales and experiences no "apprehension of any possible danger from them" (104). His main interest is money, shown as he regards Ahab's doubloon in terms of how many cigars it would purchase. Even in death, he focuses on money, thinking about this mother's need for cash: "I hope my poor mother's drawn my part-pay ere this" (506).

Ahab is not religious like Starbuck, jolly like Stubb, or mediocre like Flask. As a result, he is not as limited as his three mates.

Motifs and Symbols

Melville supports his themes, develops his characters, and corroborates his reflections by using motifs and symbols.

Moby Dick

Although Moby Dick is one of the best-known literary symbols, what he represents is an enigma, based on who is doing the interpreting. To some, like Starbuck and the one-armed captain of the *Samuel Enderby*, he is a natural animal without hatred or supernatural powers. Because he is large and dangerous, they feel he is best avoided.

To others, such as the men on the *Jeroboam*, he is the representation of God, an unknowable, all-powerful being that humans cannot understand or challenge. Many critics have embraced this view, pointing out that the White Whale, like God, cannot be known because, as Ishmael points out, his vast body is hidden in the ocean, and he is too immense to comprehend.

A number of people regard Moby Dick as a symbol for man's interpretation of the meaning of life. Melville examines the nature of the universe and man's position in it primarily by looking at Moby Dick, who is the "comprehensive dynamic symbol for the whole immense, riddling, uncaring cosmos in which man finds himself nurtured, stunned, challenged, and (if he choose and can) at home" (Parke, 68).

To Ahab, Moby Dick is the incarnation of evil, a malicious, powerful being that brings havoc on people. He feels it is his life mission to destroy this malevolent supernatural being.

Whaling Objects and Events

The most common source for Melville's symbols is found in the everyday life on board the *Pequod* as Ishmael transforms whaling items and events into abstract truths about life. Objects such as the monkey-rope and a fire under the try-pots are converted into messages about the necessity of human brotherhood and as warnings against false points of view. Incidents that occur on the trip likewise reflect life: squeezing sperm shows the need for human kindness and finding ambergris in a rotten whale exhibits unexpected sweetness in the midst of corruption. Although some of the simpler objects and events suggest only one thing, many have multiple meanings, showing the complexity and ambiguity of life.

Bigness

Critic Alfred Kazin claims that "The greatest single metaphor in the book is that of bigness" (58). In chapter after chapter, Ishmael delights in pointing out the vastness of the ocean and the immensity of the whale—its gigantic head, cavernous cavities, huge tail, substantial spinal cord, and thick blubber, which produces one hundred barrels of oil. Not only does Ishmael look at huge objects, but he also widely explores topics, such as leviathans, examining the varieties of whales, pictures and stories about whales, bodily descriptions, and living conditions; and the whaling industry, looking at the ship and boats, the watch, the chase, and the whalers' tools and duties. The "bigness" motif helps portray Melville's theme of the enormity and complexity of the universe.

Christian Motifs

From his first sentence, "Call me Ishmael" (1), to his last, "It was the devious-cruising Rachel, that in her retracing search after her missing children, only found another orphan" (509), Melville uses biblical imagery.

Doing so helps readers interpret the personalities of the two main characters, Ishmael and Ahab; two of the ships, *Jeroboam* and *Rachel*; and several minor characters. *Pequod* owner Bildad, named for Job's disapproving advisor, is satirized as a religious hypocrite who misuses the word *lay* to validate giving Ishmael a low salary, by quoting the Bible: "*Lay* not up for yourselves treasures upon earth" (69). Furthermore, both prophets are given biblical names. Elijah, named for the Old Testament prophet who was King Ahab's antagonist, hints that there may be trouble for Ishmael and Queequeg on Ahab's ship, while crazy Gabriel, who adopts the name of the messenger angel, is the ranting maniac on the *Jeroboam* who tells Ahab to quit pursuing the White Whale or God will punish him.

Melville also incorporates biblical references into the novel to examine alternative ways of thinking, as seen in the story of Jonah and the whale (Chapters 9 and 83).

However, most of Melville's Christian allusions are used to help readers visualize his characters, events, or ideas as he relates a biblical story or person to the topic he is discussing. For example, he writes that a Nantucketer's place on the sea is so ingrained that "a Noah's flood would not interrupt" it (56), and he proclaims that the Fin-Back Whale "seems the banished and unconquerable Cain of his race" (121) while the Black Fish "carries an everlasting Mephistophelean [devilish] grin on his face" (124).

The Christian references are multitudinous. Melville draws upon Old Testament celebrities; New Testament figures; biblical places; and biblical stories and references. He also includes references to Christian church leaders (St. Dominic, St. Sytlites, Dunfermline monks, Archbishop Becket) and Christian churches (Canterbury Cathedral, St. Peter's church).

Using Christian references not only gives the novel richness and depth, but it also firmly sets the book in the

Western tradition, using the religion of the founding fathers of America.

Western Historical, Mythological, and Societal Allusions
Melville also fills his novel with comparisons to well-known people, gods, and objects from Western culture. He includes historical persons, such as Caesar, Descartes, Mark Antony, Cleopatra, St. George, Columbus, King Edward, Shakespeare, Melancthon, Goethe, Michelangelo, Pythagoras, Hannibal, and Aristotle. He incorporates the mythological figures of Prometheus, Achilles, the Theban Sphinx, Jupiter's son Perseus, Hercules, and Pan. He refers to places around the world, such as Lima, Venice, Joppa of Syria, and Actium. And he selects items from various cultures, such as Egyptian mummies, Herschel's great telescope, the Roman war-chariot, and the Heidelburgh Tun.

These references, like the Christian allusions, greatly add to the novel's profundity, and they further enhance the book as a Western work of art.

American Frontier Motifs
Another motif is that of the American frontier, a place of exotic people and unusual experiences. Melville sometimes uses Native Americans as references: Ishmael insists on sailing from the old frontier town of Nantucket, where "those aboriginal whalemen, the Red-Men, first sall[ied] out in canoes to give chase to the Leviathan" (6); the *Pequod* is named for the Indian tribe massacred by the Puritans; whaling captains who search out ferocious whales do so as intently as "Captain Butler of old had it in his mind to capture that notorious murderous savage Annawon, the headmost warrior of the Indian King Philip" (183); and the whalemen paddle their boats "seated like Ontario Indians" (256). In addition to references to American Indians, Melville also makes one of his "daring harpooners," Tashtego, an "unmixed Indian" of Gay Head, a section of Martha's Vineyard (105).

Melville also uses the backwoods frontiersman—Daniel Boone, Davy Crockett, and Kit Carson—another exotic American type. He also uses frontier imagery such as when Ishmael explains that a skilled harpooner snatches his weapon "as readily from its rest as a backwoodsman swings his rifle from the wall" (261).

Melville draws upon the western American landscape and animals, comparing the whale's brow to a "prairie" (301, 309), his hump to "the humped herds of buffalo" (411), his whiteness to "the White Steed of the Prairies," "the black bisons of distant Oregon," "the desolate shifting of the windrowed snows of prairies," and "the shaking of that buffalo robe" (170, 173, 175).

Besides using frontier images, Ishmael also describes the American West. The huge Great Lakes are seen as an exciting frontier that "yield their beaches to wild barbarians, whose red painted faces flash from out their peltry wigwams" (219–220). The newly constructed Erie Canal passes "through all the wide contrasting scenery of those noble Mohawk counties" (225) and is ruled by a frontier bully, the Canaller, who "would make a fine dramatic hero, so abundantly and picturesquely wicked is he" (225).

These allusions help make Melville's work a truly American novel.

Images of Death

The *Pequod*'s voyage is a journey to death. The most common death motif is the coffin, which permeates the book from the first page to the last. Ishmael begins his tale by relating that he knows he needs to renew his soul by going to sea "whenever I find myself involuntarily pausing before coffin warehouses, and bringing up the rear of every funeral I meet" (1). In the novel's final paragraph, Ishmael tells that he was saved when "the coffin life-buoy shot lengthwise from the sea, fell over, and floated by my side" (509). In between these pages, other references to coffins appear: an innkeeper ominously named Peter Coffin puts Ishmael in a room with Queequeg, which leads to a friendship that regenerates his soul; Tashtego is almost "coffined, hearsed, and tombed" (309) in the whale's head; and Fedellah tells Ahab that "neither hearse nor coffin can be thine" (442).

Additional allusions to death become frequent in the final chapters as the *Pequod* sails closer to Moby Dick. Queequeg nearly dies. Ishmael views the Pacific as the "Potters' Fields of all four continents" (430). The Parsee foretells Ahab's death. Ghostly cries "like half-articulated wailings of the ghosts of all Herod's murdered Innocents" are heard by the sailors, sounds the old Manxman insists "were the voices of newly drowned men in the sea" (463). The sailor on the masthead falls to his death. The carpenter remaking Queequeg's coffin into a lifebuoy uses words of death: "graveyard tray," "coffins and hearses," "grave-digger," and "bier" (465, 466, 467). The *Rachel* weeps for its dead children. And the *Delight* buries a sailor. All of these strengthen the idea that the *Pequod* is heading for death.

The final day of the chase, Melville uses several death references: the two hearses, Captain Ahab's death, and the sinking ship. Even the epilogue reinforces the death images, as Ishmael is saved by the coffin life-buoy, and the sorrowful *Rachel*, searching for its dead, rescues him. Thus, at the end, death becomes a part of life.

Literary Reception of Novel

Moby Dick first appeared in England, where it was published in bowdlerized form: with some offensive sentences excised; with the etymology and extracts relegated to the back, rather than serving as a gateway to the novel; and worst of all, without the epilogue. Although some English reviewers praised *Moby Dick* as "far beyond the level of an ordinary work of fiction" with its "true philosophy," "genuine poetry," and "profound reflections," others condemned it, slamming the novel's ending in which Ishmael apparently dies. The prestigious London *Athenæum* blasted it as "trash belonging to the worst school of Bedlam literature." American readers heard about the English reviews and were thus prejudiced against the novel, even though their edition did include the epilogue. In a way, the book was doomed in the United States before it was even published because of the way in which it had been published in England. Thus, most influential American reviewers berated the book. The Boston *Post* viciously concluded that *Moby Dick* was "not worth the money asked for it, either as a literary work or as a mass of printed paper"; the *Literary World* blasted it for its "piratical running down of creeds and opinions"; while the New York *Independent* sharply warned Melville that "The Judgment day will hold him liable for not turning his talents to better account." Certainly, not all American critics condemned the novel; in fact, one New York reviewer praised Melville for writing "with the gusto of true genius" and enlivening his novel with "the raciness of his humor and the redolence of his imagination."

Readers, however, agreed with the negative critics and did not buy the book. Although 1,535 copies were sold in the first month, and another 471 by February 7, 1852, sales immediately tapered off. From 1852–1862, only 1,236 copies, averaging 123 per year, were sold. A mere 555 copies, or 23 yearly, were purchased from 1863–1887 (Hetherington, 15). For the last decades of Melville's life, *Moby Dick* was basically a forgotten book.

It was not until the 1920s that Melville's novel was recognized as a masterpiece. This happened after Raymond Weaver revived interest in Melville with the publication of his biography in 1921 and Melville's posthumous book, *Billy Budd*, in 1924. Almost immediately, the general public began to see *Moby Dick* as a timely book reflecting the troubles they were experiencing. With dictators like Adolf Hitler on the rise, readers viewed Captain Ahab as a prototype for humans' ability for hatred, treachery, and violence. Later generations have regarded the book as far more than a political reflection. Ahab, a type of everyman, has been embraced by counterculturalists, antiwar activists, environmentalists, gays and bisexuals, and multiculturalists. Since 9/11, Captain Ahab has been compared both to war advocates, such as President George W. Bush's administration, who pursue terrorists much like Ahab tirelessly tracked down Moby Dick, and to terrorists such as Osama bin Laden, who are seen as hate-filled, fanatic Ahabs.

In the academic field, *Moby Dick* is viewed as part of the U.S. literary canon, studied by high school, college, university, and graduate students. Yearly, numerous critics analyze the book, looking at it from historical, psychological, gender, cultural, and racial perspectives. Some of their essays appear in the nationally acclaimed journal devoted to Melville's works, *Leviathan*, named for Melville's whale. Scholars also gather to talk about Melville's masterpiece at conferences throughout the nation.

Because of its popularity, *Moby Dick* has been adopted into other forms, including John Huston's 1956 film starring Gregory Peck and USA's 1998 television miniseries starring Patrick Stewart. *Moby Dick* has also been filmed in German (1931), French (2004), and Japanese (1997–1999, 2005–2006). An opera version, *And God Created Great Whales*, was written by Rinde Eckert in 2000. The novel is featured in a play-within-a-play, Orson Welles' *Moby Dick—Rehearsed*; and in a musical, Robert Longden's *Moby Dick! The Musical*, the story of a girls' boarding school production of Melville's novel.

Moby Dick's exciting plot and strong characters have been borrowed by filmmakers in movies. For instance, Sam Peckinpah's 1965 film *Major Dundee* places *Moby Dick*-like characters in a Western setting, while Steven Spielberg's 1975 *Jaws*, based on Peter Benchley's novel,

USA Network produced a television miniseries of *Moby Dick* in 1998, starring Patrick Stewart as the obsessive Captain Ahab. One of the dangers of whaling is vividly portrayed in this picture as Ahab, throwing his harpoon into Moby Dick, is so close to the mighty leviathan that the whale's eye almost dwarfs the man.

includes a fanatical sea captain like Ahab who is fixated on hunting down a white shark.

Moby Dick is popular with novelists, too. As early as 1870, Jules Verne alluded to a hunt for a treacherous ship-sinking "Moby-Dick" in *20,000 Leagues Under the Sea*. A century later, two science-fiction writers borrowed Melville's ideas: in 1968 Samuel R. Delany converted Ahab into a facially scarred and obsessive starship captain in *Nova*, and in 1971 Philip José Farmer took Ishmael into the future in *The Wind Whales of Ishmael*. Using *Moby Dick* as a starting point, Sena Jeter Naslund wrote a novel in 1999 about the Captain's wife, *Ahab's Wife: Or, the Star Gazer*.

Even musicians embrace *Moby Dick*, including Melville's descendent, Richard Melville Hull, who records under the name "Moby." Many other musicians have recorded songs based on *Moby Dick*: Led Zeppelin's instrumental recording "Moby Dick"; Mountain's "Nantucket Sleighride" (depicting a ship's crew, including a man named Starbuck, searching for a sperm whale); Laurie Anderson's multimedia stage presentation, *Songs and Stories from Moby Dick*, and her CD, *Life on a String*; the heavy metal band Mastodon's 2004 album *Leviathan* (songs include "I Am Ahab" and "Seabeast"); and classical composer Francis McBeth's suite for wind band, "Of Sailors and Whales" (which includes five movements, each titled for a Melville character: Ishmael, Queequeg, Father Mapple, Ahab, The White Whale).

As a well-known icon, Melville's whale is widely used in popular culture. He is found in cartoons (MGM's 1962 Tom and Jerry meet "Dicky Moe"); in video games (the "Skies of Arcadia" has a purple whale that threatens people); as an action figure (Mattel's "Moby Lick," a killer whale with a huge tongue); and in comic books (Disney's Donald has a relative named "Moby Duck"; Marvel Comic's *Livewires* concerns a secret project called "The White Whale"; and Jeff Smith's comic book series *Bone* contains a character who causes his friends, including one with a peg-leg and facial scar, to fall asleep when he reads *Moby Dick*). In addition, the name "Moby Dick" has been adopted by commercial enterprises around the world, such as restaurants; a sight-seeing boat in Copenhagen, Denmark; and a Belgian brothel, "Moby Dick Fun Pub" (Delbanco, 8–9).

Truly Melville's novel has made a huge impact on readers, scholars, filmmakers, writers, and popular culture in America and throughout the world. The book is a magical one, admired for its stirring plot, vivid characters, eloquent language, humor and ferocity, symbolism and philosophy, and exotic descriptions of cetology.

ting plot, a multitude of facts, a wealth of philosop
ements, and a huge number of comparisons and symbols. ?
is it that experts have had trouble placing it in a

LINED WITH MASSIVE BUILDINGS, WALL STREET, THE PRISONLIKE SETTING FOR "BARTLEBY, THE SCRIVENER," FORMS THE HEART OF NEW YORK'S FINANCIAL DISTRICT. TRINITY CHURCH, WHERE THE NARRATOR WAS GOING ON THE SUNDAY HE DISCOVERED THAT BARTLEBY LIVES IN HIS LAW OFFICE, IS LOCATED AT THE TOP OF THE STREET.

c romance, a romance of the sea, a metaphysical novel,
ogical novel, a saga of the whale, and a tale of tragic
. But, as critic John D. Reeves points out, "no one cla
on says enough—a shortfall that testifies to the vast
ity of Moby Dick." He, like many others, therefore, s
s this vast work a "novel." Moby Dick, published in 1851

Chapter 5

"Bartleby, the Scrivener"

"Bartleby, the Scrivener: A Story of Wall-Street" is one of the most famous short stories written in nineteenth-century America.

Plot

The unnamed narrator is a well-established lawyer on Wall Street in New York City. He employs two scriveners, Turkey and Nippers, and a young office boy, Ginger Nut. When he decides he needs one more copyist, Bartleby, a "pallidly neat, pitiably respectable, incurably forlorn" (19) man, answers his ad. At first, Bartleby seems to be an ideal worker, but then he surprises his boss by refusing to do some work, politely stating, "I would prefer not to" (20). Increasingly, he "prefers not to" do the tasks asked of him.

One Sunday, the narrator is surprised and saddened to find that Bartleby lives at his office, a place deserted on weekends and evenings. After Bartleby refuses to do any work, the narrator first tries to get rid him, but then pities him and decides to let him remain. However, when people wonder about this strange man who loiters in his rooms, the lawyer moves his offices, leaving Bartleby behind. However, the new tenants tell the lawyer that he is responsible for Bartleby, and thus the lawyer tries to interest the scrivener in a new job and even offers him a temporary home with him. When Bartleby refuses, he is sent to prison for vagrancy where he slowly starves himself, dying just before the attorney makes a second visit to him.

After Bartleby's death, the narrator learns that Bartleby once clerked in the Dead Letter Office and assumes that this work contributed to Bartleby's depression. He sees that Bartleby is related to all humanity.

Themes and Issues
The main themes found in this story revolve around human isolation and class conflict, as embodied primarily in Bartleby, and brotherly love, as seen through the anonymous narrator.

Isolation and Alienation
Isolated from all living things, Bartleby is one of the loneliest characters ever created. He is cut off from the natural world, living and working in an office on Wall Street, a bleak place with tall brick buildings that hem people in. The lawyer's prisonlike office is a cheerless, lifeless place with windows on one side that open into a light shaft and on the other side that look out on brick walls. Bartleby is also disconnected from other humans, existing in the empty office that lies on a street that is deserted on nights and weekends. All alone in the world, with no family or friends, except the narrator, Bartleby lives a death-in-life existence.

Class Conflict and the Nature of the Workplace
Although Melville does not give any reasons for Bartleby's estrangement, Marxist critics argue that Bartleby's isolation is a result of being an alienated worker in the financial world of Wall Street. In this business atmosphere, people lose their humanity as they become part of the necessary machinery that keeps businesses going. So impersonal is this place that the narrator does not even have a name; his original employees—Turkey, Nippers, and Ginger Nut—are only called by their nicknames; and Bartleby, identified as a worker (a "scrivener"), has only a

surname. Since Bartleby cannot force himself to keep trying to survive in this emotionally dead world, he quits
working step by step, disassociating himself from it until
he dies physically.

This Marxist view of the story has been somewhat dis-
credited by critics who note that the narrator is not a
heartless capitalist because he pays Bartleby a salary after
he refuses to work and offers to help him. Furthermore,
many aspects of the tale, such as the Dead Letter Office
conclusion and Bartleby's refusals to do many things
besides working, do not fit the idea that Bartleby is a parable of an alienated worker. Instead, historical critics con-
tend that Melville, knowing that Wall Street was filled
with labor activists in the 1840s and 1850s, purposely set
his story there to make a statement about class struggle
(Kuebrich, 382–384). The lawyer uses his position as an
employer to "legitimate inequality and class privilege,"
while "Bartleby's principled refusal to work . . . is a
response to the impersonal, unequal, and exploitative
working conditions that were inspiring an organized
working class resistance" (Kuebrich, 386).

Brotherly Love

Through the narrator, Melville explores the relationships
between people and the extent to which they should help
others. When the narrator quotes the Biblical command to
"love one another" (36) and refers to all humans as the
"sons of Adam" (28), Melville is clearly showing the common bonds of humanity which unite all people. However,
the author also illustrates that Christianity's highest ideals
of showing total love to others can rarely, if ever, be ful-
filled. Although the lawyer repeatedly tries to help Bartleby,
he often does so for selfish reasons. Furthermore, his good
deeds go unrewarded, for Bartleby dies.

The theme of Christian responsibility is not just the
story of one man; it "is also a meditation on a large moral

issue: . . . how to define collective responsibility"
(Delbanco, 220) for the unfortunate, the poor, and the
alienated members of society. Although Melville shows
that people owe fellow human beings love and charity, he
integrates this "with the psychological and social truth
that sympathy and benevolence have their limits"
(Delbanco, 221).

Analysis
Characters
As Walter E. Anderson contends, how "Bartleby, the Scrivener" is interpreted "crucially depends upon the attitude
taken towards both the lawyer and Bartleby" (384). Critics
have offered highly contradictory views of both men.

Bartleby
Until recently, most scholars have focused on Bartleby as
the main character of the story, primarily examining his
motives for preferring not to act. Although all of them recognize that Bartleby is an alienated individual, they do not
agree on the reasons for his estrangement. Scholars offer
five main interpretations of the character of Bartleby.

First are those critics who regard Bartleby as a biographical portrait of Melville as a nonconforming artist.
The scrivener, they perceive, represents a literary artist like
Melville who, unable to sell the type of books he wants
to write, refuses to create the kind of fiction demanded
for commercial success. Second are the Marxists who consider Bartleby an alienated worker who refuses to work in
a capitalistic prison. Since the story takes place on Wall
Street, the financial center of the country, these scholars
see Bartleby's refusals as a criticism of the growing mate-
rialism in America. To them, Bartleby is a hero who rejects
the economic world. The third interpretation is offered by
those who look upon the story historically, seeing Bartleby
as a representative of alienated workers of New York City

in the mid-nineteenth century. These three schools of thought promote Bartleby as a victim of people who either cannot appreciate him or exploit him for their own profit. The other two schools of thought offer broader interpretations of Bartleby, regarding him as representative of all humans. The fourth critical group finds that Bartleby is alienated from normal American society because of sickness. One critic contends that this separation occurs because Bartleby is a schizophrenic (Beja, 555–568), while another says that the world, not Bartleby, is sick. Therefore, the copyist, seeing the total "meaninglessness of the universe" refuses to work or even live in the world because "there is no possibility of meaningful action" (Dillingham, 47).

The final interpretation revolves around Bartleby as a Christ-figure whose "mission is divine: to awaken the narrator to his responsibility with regard to the keeping of his brother" (Forst, 266). These analysts believe Bartleby is isolated because those in society deny him charity and therefore fail in their Christian duty.

In spite of all the essays written on the scrivener, no one has been able to definitively characterize Bartleby because, as Todd F. Davis points out, none of these analyses "draws its interpretations solely from the text. Rather it appears that all impose meaning or meaninglessness upon Bartleby" (186). There is not much in the text to describe him; Bartleby speaks little, does little, and offers no clues for his motives. The copyist's polite but firm refusal, "I would prefer not to," has puzzled people since the story was first printed, and Bartleby remains an enigma.

Narrator-Lawyer

In recent years, a number of scholars have come to recognize that it is the anonymous narrator, not Bartleby, who is the chief character in the story, and that the story is "a drama of testing" (Furlani, 353) of the lawyer. How the attorney responds to the reclusive Bartleby and meets this "most provoking test of brotherhood" (Schechter, 360) is the subject of much debate.

Some critics look upon the narrator as a self-interested man who fails in his Christian duty of love, comparing him to Biblical figures such as Judas (Stein, 107), and Pontius Pilate (Eliot, 11). They argue that even though the narrator tries to act with Christian love, he is only a "superficially charitable" (Morgan, 263) hypocrite and his acts are filled with "a distinct element of self-interest" (Schechter, 360). However, these negative views of the lawyer do not seem accurate, for, as other interpreters have pointed out, the attorney takes great measures to help Bartleby, efforts so virtuous that they amount to "heroism" (Craver and Plante, 133–134). Although this decent man first "resembles the self-satisfied Pharisee in Jesus' story (Luke 18:9–11)" (Morgan, 257), he grows as the story progresses, losing his complacency as he becomes concerned for the welfare of Bartleby and follows the Christian mandate to be his brother's keeper.

At the beginning of the tale, the Wall Street lawyer acts out of self-interest by following "the easiest way of life" (14). First, he ignores Bartleby's refusals to do tasks. But, when Bartleby's passive resistance "aggravates" him (23), he decides to treat him charitably in order to "purchase a delicious self-approval . . . [which] will cost me little or nothing, while I lay up in my soul what will eventually prove a sweet morsel for my conscience" (23–24).

In his next stage he teeters back and forth between true charity and self-interest. This begins after he discovers that Bartleby lives in his office, causing him to feel "sincerest pity" (29) because he recognizes the "bond of a common humanity" that joins Bartleby and him as "sons of Adam" (28). But soon this empathy turns to "repulsion" (29), when he understands that he cannot help Bartleby: "I might give alms to his body; but his body did not pain him; it was his soul that suffered, and his soul I could not reach" (29). Therefore, he tries to get rid of Bartleby by bribing him with his wages plus a $20 bonus, a large amount of money in the nineteenth century. When this does not work, the lawyer determines to follow Jesus' command to "love one another" (36) and let Bartleby live in his office. This resolution lasts until Bartleby's idleness threatens his reputation; then he decides to rid himself of Bartleby forever by relocating his offices. However, he soon learns that he cannot abandon his spiritual duties so easily, for the new tenants tell him he is responsible for the man he left behind. Although he three times tries to deny his responsibility by stating that "the man you allude to is nothing to me" (39), he does finally agree to visit Bartleby because he is "fearful" of "being exposed in the papers" (40). Once more he unsuccessfully tries to befriend the lonely man, suggesting alternative employments and even offering him a place to live at his home.

His last acts of love to Bartleby—visiting him in prison, calling him his friend, and feeding him—are done solely out of charity. By the end of the story, this very human lawyer muses on the effects the Dead Letter Office had on Bartleby and recognizes Bartleby's brotherhood with all humanity: "Ah Bartleby! Ah humanity!" (45).

Motifs and Symbols
Motifs and symbols are used throughout the story to develop themes.

Walls
Melville uses walls, which cut people off from others, to help develop the theme of isolation. In life, Bartleby is isolated by the screens and walls of the office on Wall Street, and in death, by the prison wall.

Death

To help portray the theme of human isolation, Bartleby, so isolated that he is "dead-in-life" (Hoag, 127), is described as a ghost and a corpse. When the scrivener first appears, he looks ghostlike—"A motionless young man" (19) who works "silently, palely, mechanically" (20). A few days later, he appears "Like a very ghost" when the lawyer roars his name (25). He haunts the building after work hours, living in the office and appearing as an "apparition" (26) when the lawyer visits his office on a Sunday. More than a ghost, Bartleby is also a corpse, who greets the attorney on that Sunday with "his cadaverously gentlemanly *nonchalance*" (27). When he refuses to work, his "mildly cadaverous reply" is, "I would prefer not to" (30). This image of Bartleby as a living dead man continues to the very end of the story in which he is seen as a type of dead letter (Weinstock, 23; Zlogar, 507–508).

Classical Allusions

Critic Thomas Dilworth (52–54) points out several classical allusions that relate to the themes of isolation and brotherly love. Isolation is seen when the lawyer, learning that Bartleby lives in the office, compares the deserted Wall Street to "Petra" (27), an Arab city abandoned when Rome conquered the area in 106 CE, and views Bartleby as "a sort of innocent and transformed Marius" (28), the Roman general exiled to Carthage. Brotherly love is connected to the lawyer's bust of Cicero, the Roman lawyer who wrote a treatise on friendship. When Bartleby refuses to work, the lawyer cannot consider firing him, stating, "I should have as soon thought of turning my pale plaster-of-paris bust Cicero out of doors" (21). He refers to this bust again after Bartleby has stopped doing all work, noting that Bartleby kept his eyes "fixed upon my bust of Cicero" (30). These references help emphasize Bartleby's isolation and the lawyer's need to show compassion.

Christian and Biblical Allusions
Biblical references all portray the theme of brotherhood. Old Testament references to "Adam" (28, 36) and the ending quote from the Book of Job, Bartleby sleeps "with kings and counselors" (45), refer to the solidarity of all people. Christian allusions—Trinity Church where Christian values are taught (26, 29), charity (23, 36, 37), and Jesus' commandment to love one another (36)—all deal with the Christian virtue of love.

Literary Reception of Story

From the beginning, Melville's tale of Bartleby was commended. In 1853, the editors of *Putnam's Monthly Magazine* liked the story so much that they paid Melville five dollars per page when the standard rate was three dollars (Sealts, 484).

The story was reprinted in *The Piazza Tales* in 1856, a book which was widely reviewed and "manifestly pleased his critics" (Sealts, 501). A number of reviewers felt that "Bartleby" was the best of the stories, calling it "the most original story in the volume," and "one of the best bits of writing which ever came from the author's pen."

In the twentieth century, "Bartleby the Scrivener" became one of Melville's most popular and most famous works, hailed as "a prime example of Melville's finest work" (Hillway, 139). Anthologized in high school, college, and university texts, it is read by huge numbers of students. It has been made into a number of films, including Jonathan Parker's 2001 *Bartleby*, starring Crispin Glover and David Paymer. Countless scholars have analyzed it; in fact, so much has been written on "Bartleby" that Dan McCall, writing in 1989, calls these critics "the Bartleby Industry" (x). With its theme of alienation, many analysts have regarded it as a forerunner to Existentialist and Absurdist literature of the twentieth century.

SOME OF MELVILLE'S MOST FAMOUS STORIES WERE FIRST PUBLISHED IN
PUTNAM'S MONTHLY MAGAZINE, INCLUDING FIVE OF THE SIX WORKS
THAT WERE COLLECTED IN *THE PIAZZA TALES*. MELVILLE'S NOVEL
ISRAEL POTTER: HIS FIFTY YEARS OF EXILE, WHICH ALSO FIRST
APPEARED IN *PUTNAM'S*, IS PICTURED HERE.

More than one hundred fifty years after its publication, "Bartleby the Scrivener," along with *Moby Dick* and *Billy Budd*, form "the trio of Melville's most revered work" (Hardwick, 110).

ting plot, a multitude of facts, a wealth of philosop
ements, and a huge number of comparisons and symbols. S
is it that experts have had trouble placing it in a
genre

IN THE 1962 BRITISH FILM VERSION OF BILLY BUDD, DIRECTED BY PETER
USTINOV, TERENCE STAMP STARS AS THE HONORABLE BILLY. SOMETIMES
UNABLE TO SPEAK BECAUSE OF A STAMMER, BILLY USES HIS FISTS TO EXPRESS
HIMSELF, AN ACTION WHICH LEADS TO HIS ACCIDENTAL MURDER OF THE
SADISTIC MASTER-AT-ARMS, JOHN CLAGGART.

prose epic, a prose allegory, an extended prose poem, a
romance, a romance of the sea, a metaphysical novel,
gical novel, a saga of the whale, and a tale of tragic
But, as critic John D. Reeves points out, "no one cla
says enough—a shortfall that testifies to the vast
ity of Moby Dick." He, like many others, therefore,
this vast work a "novel." Moby Dick, published in 1851

Chapter 6

Billy Budd, Sailor (An Inside Narrative)

Because *Billy Budd* was left as a working manuscript when Melville died in 1891, the original text is hard to follow with its crossed-out words, alternate word choices, and unclear chapter breaks. As a result, there are different versions and different titles of this book. Discovered and published in 1924 and revised in 1928 by biographer Raymond Weaver, it was first titled *Billy Budd, Foretopman*. In 1948, F. Barron Freeman issued a new version, *Billy Budd (An Inside Narrative)*, which was revised in 1956 by Elizabeth Treeman. In the 1950s, Harrison Hayford and Merton M. Sealts Jr. revisited Melville's original text and found that the early versions contained numerous errors, including title, names of ships, quotations at the heads of chapters, chapter divisions, word choices, and ordering of material. In 1962 the University of Chicago published their book, which is considered the definitive edition: *Billy Budd, Sailor (An Inside Narrative)*.

Plot

In 1797, when Britain is at war with France, Billy Budd, a handsome, naïve sailor on a merchant ship, is forced to join the British Navy aboard a warship. Here he is well-liked by everyone except the master-at-arms, John Claggart, who falsely accuses him of trying to start a mutiny. Captain Vere does not believe the charges and urges Billy to defend himself. Unable to speak because of a stutter, Billy Budd punches Claggart in the forehead, killing him immediately. Although Captain Vere sympathizes with Billy, he feels he must follow the naval rules exactly. Therefore, he calls in three men for a court martial and argues that Billy must hang because he killed a ship officer. When the men suggest that he pardon Billy, the Captain convinces them that doing so would tempt the crew to mutiny. Therefore, Billy is condemned to be hung the next morning. Although the sailors are grief-stricken, Billy does not resent the Captain and dies blessing him.

Three episodes conclude the book. Captain Vere, wounded in battle, dies murmuring Billy's name. The official report of Billy's hanging exonerates Claggart and casts Billy as a mutineer. The sailors revere Billy, regarding the yardarm he was hung from as a relic.

Themes and Issues

Melville changes his themes as he develops this story. Focusing primarily on Billy and Claggart, he begins with a theological study of the Fall of Man. Then, centering his story on Captain Vere, he studies imperfect human beings as they attempt to achieve justice. His tale concludes with a look at the nature of truth.

The Conflict Between Good and Evil

Biographer Newton Arvin accurately describes the story of Billy Budd as a "fable of the Fall of Man, the loss of Paradise" (294). The Handsome Sailor is a type of noble savage, an innocent Adam before the fall (52), but he has one blemish, a stutter. Juxtaposed to him is the Satanic figure, the "snake" (99) John Claggart, whose evilness is "a depravity according to nature" (76). Envious of Billy not only because of his "good looks, cheery health, and frank enjoyment of young life" (78), but also because of his moral nature that "never willed malice or experienced the reactionary bite of that serpent" (78), the master-at-arms, like the serpent Satan in the Garden of Eden, cunningly takes away Billy's innocence and happiness.

The Difficulty in Achieving Justice

Melville examines how difficult it is for ordinary human beings to grant true justice because often there is no absolute right and wrong. Some critics have suggested that Melville was especially interested in this topic because his cousin, Guert Gansevoort, a lieutenant on board the *Somers* in 1842, was head of a council which decided that, for the safety of the ship, three sailors needed to be hanged for conspiracy to mutiny. The decision was highly controversial, and Melville's cousin was haunted by the decision for years.

In *Billy Budd*, it is Captain Vere who must attempt to make a fair decision about Billy's destiny. Ideally, Vere could pardon Billy and yet maintain control of his crew like the superlative leader, Admiral Horatio Nelson, who wins over his crew "by force of his mere presence and heroic personality" (59). But the captain of the *Bellipotent* is an ordinary, limited man who cannot lead people by example. Therefore, he decides that it is prudent to hang Billy so no other sailor will dare mutiny. Although Melville carefully delineates Vere's just reasons for executing Billy—military law and fear of mutiny—he also shows that this is a "terribly flawed solution" (Hunt, 288) because an innocent person is sacrificed. This novel, therefore, shows "the inescapably dilemmatic nature of certain choices. It alleges the impossibility of resolving them in any comfortable way" (Hunt, 273).

The Rights of the Individual versus the Needs of the State

The theme of individual rights in conflict with the needs of a government at war begins immediately as Billy is impressed onto a naval ship, a legalized form of kidnapping, in order to staff a warship. That Billy's rights are usurped is clear when he innocently bids farewell to the merchant ship, "And good-bye to you too, old *Rights-of-Man*" (49). This theme is further developed when the naval captain, enforcing naval rules set up to insure military stability, orders the death penalty on innocent Billy. This theme is especially pertinent today, as post-9/11 Americans try to balance individual rights with the safety of the nation.

The Need for Forgiveness and Acceptance

Although Melville shows that evil is a destroying presence in the world, he also illustrates that people can face tragedy with generosity. This is seen first with Captain Vere who honorably takes full responsibility for his decision as he visits Billy to personally tell him why he has condemned him to death. It is even more poignant in Billy, who generously forgives his judge as he calls out, "God bless Captain Vere!" (123). Billy shows that peace and forgiveness are possible even when evil triumphs.

The Nature of Truth

When Melville writes that "truth uncompromisingly told will always have its ragged edges" (128), he is explaining that absolute truth and certainty are often unreachable. The difficulty of determining the truth of whether or not Billy's death was necessary is seen in the contradictory stories and emotions portrayed in the "inside narrative" and in the three conclusions to the history of Billy Budd. The "inside narrative" ends with three different valid responses to Billy's execution: the stoicism of the dutiful Captain who shows no emotion as he stands "erectly rigid" (124); the outrage of the sailors who smother their conscience-based protests; and the acceptance of Billy, who forgives and blesses his condemner.

The concluding episodes contradict one another, once more showing the impossibility of achieving truth. In the first, Captain Vere's dying words, "Billy Budd, Billy Budd" (129), do not clarify Vere's attitude. Although they are not regarded by the attendant as "the accents of remorse"

(129), Vere's words could be an expression of guilt, but they could also be a sigh of regret that he was forced to condemn a good man. Although the second episode, the naval report, upholds the Captain's decision to follow military law, it misrepresents the characters of Billy and Claggart. Readers are appalled to read the unjust accusations that the "criminal," Billy, in "extreme depravity" "vindictively stabbed" the "respectable and discreet" (130) master-at-arms. The third episode, the reaction of the sailors, shows the great pity they feel for wronged Billy Budd, whom they revere as a type of Christ figure.

As a result of these conflicting episodes, readers have a hard time determining what truth Melville is trying to portray. For decades, critics described *Billy Budd* as Melville's "last will and testament," but they disagreed on the nature of his testament. Some early critics found it a "testament of acceptance," claiming that Melville no longer blamed God for evil but recognized it as a necessary condition of life. Contrarily, many later scholars proclaimed the book a "testament of resistance" (Withim, 78), arguing that Melville was protesting against evil and injustice.

In recent decades, the debate about Melville's intended truth has switched from focusing on Melville's spiritual state to examining Captain Vere. Those who view the Captain as a despot who "invoked 'national security' to cover politically expedient violations of civil rights" (Robertson-Lorant, 594) believe Melville is trying to convey truths about the brutality of the modern state, but others defend Vere as "an anguished but duty-bound representative of the political state" (Milder, xxxvi) who did what was necessary to maintain order and discipline in a dangerous world. They think Melville is showing the necessity of individual sacrifice for the good of the many.

Obviously readers have not reached consensus about the truth Melville is relating. Instead of accepting or protesting, Melville seems to show that "the possibilities of truth [are] too elusive for him—or any intelligent person for that matter—to settle on a position" (Yannella, 6). In fact, Lester H. Hunt argues that "*Billy Budd* is a determined attempt to prevent us from coming to rest in the comfort of a solution" (293–294).

Analysis

Because of the moral dilemma presented in *Billy Budd*, the personalities and roles of the three main characters have received much attention.

Characters

Billy Budd

Most readers regard the title character as a representative of the almost ideal human. Physically, he is nearly perfect —a blonde, blue-eyed, twenty-one-year-old handsome man with a perfect build and a beautiful complexion who is so physically alluring that he is compared to Hercules (51), Apollo (48), Achilles (71), and Alexander (44). His major flaw is a stutter, brought on when he is upset. His inner qualities match his outward appearance. A natural peacemaker, a respectful comrade, and a happy person, he is a very popular man. His most apparent characteristic is his innocence. Like Adam, Billy is a simple, pure, trusting man who has no knowledge of evil.

So good is he that his death is compared to Christ's crucifixion: "the vapory fleece" like "the fleece of the Lamb of God" shines "with a soft glory" as "Billy ascended" (124). Miraculously, his body makes no movement, a sign of divine intervention. For years after his death, Billy is venerated like Christ. The sailors cherish a fragment from the spar from which Billy was hung as "a piece of the Cross" (131), and they sing a ballad about him (132). Billy is seen as an innocent Christlike man unjustly accused and executed.

However, seeing Billy as a nearly perfect man may not be the way Melville views him, for, in spite of all his wonderful qualities, Billy is not totally ideal. First, he lacks many of Christ's positive characteristics; he is violent, illiterate, ignorant of good and evil, and simpleminded. Furthermore, although he is compared to various classical heroes who possess "strength and beauty" (44), these heroes also have negative characteristics which could be associated with Billy. For example, Achilles has a weak spot, his heel, just as Billy has a defect, his stammer; and Hercules becomes violent, insanely killing his two children, just as Billy becomes violent, punching and killing Claggart. By comparing Billy to flawed characters, Melville may be implying that his title character is not ideal.

John Claggart

The master-at-arms is "a sinister character who has much in common with Satan" (Thompson, 360). This unpopular, thirty-five-year-old chief of the secret police is a man filled with "elemental evil" (78) which was "born with him and innate" (76). Jealous of Billy's physical beauty and moral goodness, he works to destroy Billy. Although Melville is clear that Claggart is envious of both Billy's innate goodness and his physical perfection, some critics have proclaimed that his jealousy is caused solely because of the sailor's handsome body. These writers see homosexuality as a main topic in *Billy Budd*, suggesting that Claggart, sexually attracted to Billy, wants to destroy him. However, this view goes against Melville's statement that Claggart's depravity "partakes nothing of the sordid or sensual" (76).

Captain Edward Fairfax Vere

Vere, Latin for "truth," is the intellectual, serious, cautious, middle-aged captain of the *Bellipotent* who obediently serves the King. He has been seen by readers as either a hero or a villain for his execution of Billy Budd after he accidentally kills his false accuser. Many see

PETER USTINOV PLAYS THE CONFLICTED CAPTAIN VERE IN THE 1962 FILM *BILLY BUDD*. TO MAINTAIN ORDER WITH THE SAILORS DURING WARTIME, THE CAPTAIN DECIDES THAT BILLY MUST BE PUT TO DEATH BY HANGING AFTER HE UNINTENTIONALLY KILLS THE MASTER-AT-ARMS.

Captain Vere as an honorable, rational, dutiful man forced to perform a repulsive act because of a war. During times of conflict, they argue, the rights of an individual must be given up for the general good. His sacrifice of Billy "demonstrates a right response to popular violence, when the times are revolutionary" (Reynolds, 43). In the opposite camp are those who condemn Vere as a coward who could have, and should have, prevented Billy's death, but instead he is a "complacent, fascistic oppressor" (Wenke, 115). In a total miscarriage of justice, he acts as witness, prosecutor, judge, and executioner.

Melville himself does not either completely condone or condemn Vere; instead, as scholar Hunt asserts, "Melville unflinchingly represents to us the moral horror of what Captain Vere does to Billy, and yet he also depicts Vere himself with a respect that borders on admiration" (273).

Setting

Billy Budd takes place on the ship, the *Bellipotent*, in 1797 during the Napoleonic Wars, a time when Britain urgently needed additional sailors to work on the war ships. As a result, naval officers were able to stop private ships and impress men into service for the state. Just before the story takes place, two mutinies had occurred on naval ships, causing the government to pass laws that allowed naval officers to quickly and harshly deal with mutinous sailors.

Point of View

The narrator is an intelligent man, with a strong knowledge of the Bible and of mythology, who, for the most part, refuses to make judgments. His point of view changes throughout the story. Sometimes he relates his observations about people or events, such as when he is describing Admiral Nelson. Other times he seems to enter the minds of his characters, as seen when he relays Claggart's secret thoughts about Billy. Still other times, he absents himself from the action, such as when he omits the scene between Vere and Billy. Because of this changing point of view, readers are forced to actively participate in the story and make their own decisions.

Structure

The main story line follows an orderly progression: an impressed sailor is falsely charged with mutiny; he instinctively punches his accuser and accidentally kills him; the ship's captain determines that he must hang; the sailor is remembered long after he is dead. Mingled within this story, however, are a number of digressions and long character descriptions. The tale concludes with three very different responses to Billy's death. Although the book is not symmetrical, everything ties together to make a thoughtful and poignant story.

Literary Reception of Novel

Because of the renewed interest in Melville as a writer, *Billy Budd* became a classic almost as soon as it was published in 1924. It was hailed as a masterpiece by such famous writers as W. H. Auden, E. M. Forster, Albert Camus, and Thomas Mann, who called it "the most beautiful story in the world" (quoted in Delbanco, 321).

Melville's posthumous book has found its way into new forms. In 1949, Louis O. Coxe and Robert H. Chapman turned it into a stage play, *Uniform of Flesh*, renaming it *Billy Budd* in 1951. Also appearing in 1949 was the opera *Billy Budd*, with text by Salvatore Quasimodo and music by Giorgio Ghedini. Probably the most celebrated adaptation was made by England's famous composer, Benjamin Britten, who wrote a four-act opera in 1951. This work is still popular today, performed in the twenty-first century by such companies as the Lyric Opera of Chicago, the English National Opera, the Vienna State Opera, and the Washington (National) Opera. Britten's operatic version has been filmed three times, in both English and French. Also appearing in the 1950s were two television shows, one in 1955, the other in 1959. The best known film version of *Billy Budd* is the 1962 British movie directed by Peter Ustinov.

Billy Budd has been memorialized by two poets: Auden in "Herman Melville," published in 1940, and Helen Pinkerton in "Billy Budd," which appeared in 1968.

At the present time, enthusiasm for *Billy Budd* has not waned. It is one of the most anthologized stories in American literature, studied by high school, college, and graduate students. Scholars continue to analyze the work, publishing a multitude of essays yearly. And readers are still profoundly moved by the disturbing story of Billy Budd.

.ing plot, a multitude of facts, a wealth of philosop
ments, and a huge number of comparisons and symbols. S
is it that experts have had trouble placing it in a lit

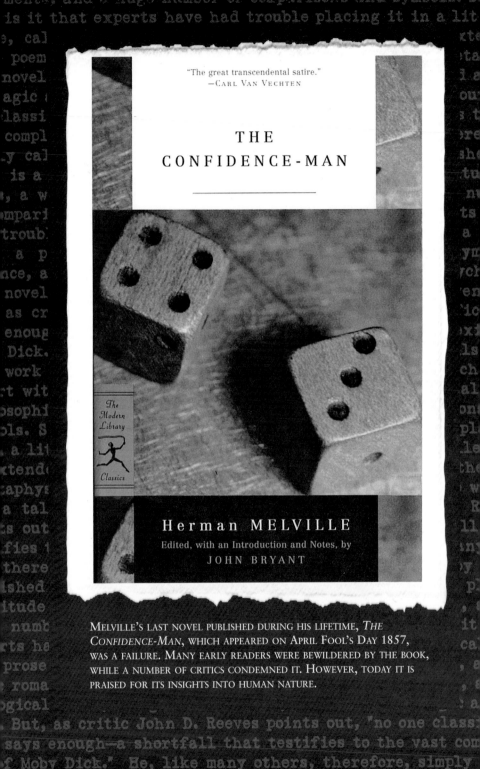

"The great transcendental satire."
—CARL VAN VECHTEN

THE CONFIDENCE-MAN

Herman MELVILLE

Edited, with an Introduction and Notes, by
JOHN BRYANT

MELVILLE'S LAST NOVEL PUBLISHED DURING HIS LIFETIME, THE CONFIDENCE-MAN, WHICH APPEARED ON APRIL FOOL'S DAY 1857, WAS A FAILURE. MANY EARLY READERS WERE BEWILDERED BY THE BOOK, WHILE A NUMBER OF CRITICS CONDEMNED IT. HOWEVER, TODAY IT IS PRAISED FOR ITS INSIGHTS INTO HUMAN NATURE.

But, as critic John D. Reeves points out, "no one class
says enough—a shortfall that testifies to the vast com
f Moby Dick." He, like many others, therefore, simply
vast work a "novel." Moby Dick, published in 1851, is a

Chapter 7

Melville's Place in Literature

WHEN HERMAN MELVILLE DIED IN 1891, he was practically forgotten as a writer, having hardly published anything the last half of his life. His most recently printed novel, *The Confidence-Man*, had appeared thirty-four years earlier, and only two volumes of poetry had been made public, one in 1866 and the other in 1876.

Melville had bloomed early as an author. When his first book, *Typee: A Peep at Polynesian Life*, was published in 1846, when he was twenty-six years old, everyone wanted to read and talk about it. As biographer Newton Arvin says, it was "a sensational success" (4), and it pushed Melville into the national spotlight as a sex symbol. Although some questioned the book's truthfulness, most readers did not care if it was fact or fiction because they liked the well-developed characters, exciting plot, and exotic setting. Melville's sequel, *Omoo*, which appeared the following year, met with the same enthusiasm. People eagerly read the mostly happy, highly adventurous tales of the South Sea Islands.

But when the young author decided to do more than entertain his readers with travel romances, his audience did not respond enthusiastically, and Melville lost his sexual appeal. Therefore, his next book, *Mardi*, a serious work which did not receive critical or public accolades, was not a financial success. Biographer Laurie Robertson-Lorant explains that "For every reader who found *Mardi* original and refreshing, there were two who found it wearisome, pedantic, and grotesque" (193).

Redburn (November 1849) and *White-Jacket* (March 1850), hastily written novels produced to make money, were better accepted by the public, but the author did not like them. In his journal on November 6, 1849, Melville called *Redburn* "trash" that he wrote "to buy some tobacco with" (Leyda, 1: 327). Although Melville had high hopes for *Moby Dick*, the novel did not bring him the public approval he desired, mostly because it was, biographer Andrew Delbanco explains, "really two books—a going-to-sea story, and a daring metaphysical adventure" (6). By 1887, fewer than four thousand copies of the novel had been sold (Hetherington, 15).

In spite of the extremely disappointing response to this book, Melville kept writing, producing an even more unsuccessful novel, *Pierre*, which was so unpopular that Melville was condemned as a writer and even regarded as insane. However, Melville still hoped to earn a living by writing, so he published stories and sketches in popular monthly magazines. Some of these works he collected as a group of stories in *The Piazza Tales*, and another, *Israel Potter*, was also published in book form. However, neither sold well. In 1857, when *The Confidence-Man* was condemned, Melville gave up writing prose pieces that the public would not buy.

His later works were written in verse. Only one, *Battle-Pieces and Aspects of the War* (1866), was commercially published, but it did not sell well. Consequently, Melville's three later collections of poetry—*Clarel* (1876), *John Marr and Other Sailors* (1888), and *Timoleon* (1891)—were paid for by private funds and were printed in limited quantities.

With the exception of Melville's first two novels, none of his writings brought him the fame, the prestige, or money he had hoped for. Publicly he was a failure, a writer who earned only a little over $10,000 for all of his books (Delbanco, 7). With his works forgotten, his death was hardly noticed, and Melville was regarded as a minor figure in American literature.

However, Americans rediscovered the artistic genius of Herman Melville in the 1920s, largely through the efforts of Raymond Weaver who, in 1921, wrote a biography, *Herman Melville, Mariner and Mystic*, and in 1924 edited and published the first copy of *Billy Budd* with the help of Melville's granddaughter. Immediately, readers looked upon Melville as a modern, innovative author. Having just witnessed the devastating results of World War I, the Jazz Agers looked upon Melville as a disillusioned man who understood evil humans. They also embraced him as a fellow rebel, a man who broke out of a prudish, confining society; as a modern psychological writer who understood the ideas popularized by Sigmund Freud; and as a man accurately disillusioned with humans.

Another cause of the Melville revival was the new feeling of national literary identity in America. People searched for good, largely unrecognized American authors and found Melville. Thus, during the 1920s, Melville became recognized as a prominent American writer, acknowledged by prominent literary historians, such as Vernon L. Parrington; and by well-known writers, including D. H. Lawrence. Melville became very famous in 1926 when Warner Brothers produced *The Sea Beast*, a movie based on *Moby Dick*. By the end of the decade, two more biographies had been written on him: John Freeman's *Herman Melville* (1926) and Lewis Mumford's *Herman Melville: A Study of His Life and Vision* (1929).

The next decades brought Melville an even greater reputation. By midcentury, a number of important critical and biographical books were published, including Newton Arvin's acclaimed *Herman Melville* (1950) and Jay Leyda's *The Melville Log: A Documentary Life of Herman Melville, 1819–1891* (1951).

Since the 1920s, Melville has been acknowledged as a major American writer. As a result, there has been a plethora of research on Melville's works and life as critics examine his writings from a variety of points of view, including Marxist, Freudian, religious, political, and historical. They have argued that Melville's fiction depicts psychological statements about homosexuality, lust, fear of sex, oedipal complexes, unhappy marriages, poverty, and pretensions. So important is Melville to scholars that they have created a Melville Society; they analyze and discuss his works in numerous literary journals, including one dedicated solely to Melville—*Leviathan*—and they attend academic conferences on Melville throughout the country.

Three recent biographies have confirmed Melville's position as an eminent figure in American fiction: Laurie Robertson-Lorant's *Melville: A Biography* (1996); Hershel Parker's *Herman Melville: A Biography*, volumes 1 and 2 (1996, 2002); and Andrew Delbanco's *Melville: His World and Work* (2005).

In high schools, colleges, and universities across the country, students study Melville's works, especially *Moby Dick*, which is, according to literary scholar Michael T. Gilmore, "the unavoidable centerpiece of the American tradition" (quoted in Delbanco, 8). As a result of their popularity, there are huge numbers of editions, printings, and translations of Melville's novels.

Not only are Melville's works highly regarded by literary experts and students, but they have been adopted by musicians, playwrights, novelists, and filmmakers. In particular, Melville's masterpiece and his greatest claim to fame, *Moby Dick*, has had numerous adaptations in film, television, stage, and opera. It has been incorporated as major parts of a play, a musical, and a variety of books. Furthermore, its plot and characters are reworked into new movies, television shows, and novels. *Billy Budd*, also regarded as a classic since its publication, has been adapted to stage, film, opera and television. Other Melville works have also been made into films in various languages. In addition, documentaries have been made on the author's life and on a true story of Moby Dick, the sinking of the ship *Essex*.

Not only are Melville's works popular in the arts, they are also admired by throngs of readers who see Melville's characters a models of their own beliefs. Captain Ahab has been embraced as a model for a number of different types of human beings, including dictators, war advocates, and antiwar activists. *Billy Budd*'s Captain Vere has been seen both as a model hero who understands the need of human sacrifice in times of war and as an oppressive tyrant. And Bartleby has been regarded as a nonconforming artist, an oppressed worker, an alienated worker in a capitalistic society, an alienated individual in a mass culture, and a type of Christ-figure who tries to awaken others to their sense of brotherly love.

Melville has also been embraced in popular culture. Largely because of *Moby Dick*, Melville has become "an American icon to a degree unmatched by any other writer" (Delbanco, 7–9). In particular, the name "Moby Dick" has been used numerous times—in cartoons, videos, comic books, songs, restaurants, and theme parks. So fashionable is Melville that on August 1, 1984, his picture was issued on a twenty-cent commemorative postage stamp.

As a result of his popularity, Melville's Pittsfield home, Arrowhead, purchased in 1975 by the Berkshire County Historical Society, has been made into a museum. It was here that the author wrote his masterpiece, *Moby Dick*, and three other novels, *Pierre*, *The Confidence-Man*, and *Israel Potter*, as well as his short story collection, *The Piazza Tales*, all of his magazine stories, and some of his poetry. In 1953, Pittsfield's public library, the Berkshire Athenaeum, dedicated a room to the famous author, the

BENITO CERENO

BY HERMAN MELVILLE

WITH PICTURES BY E. McKNIGHT KAUFFER

MCMXXVI

THE NONESUCH PRESS
16 GREAT JAMES STREET, LONDON

IN 1926, DURING THE TIME OF THE MELVILLE REVIVAL, NONESUCH PRESS PRINTED A BEAUTIFUL EDITION OF BENITO CERENO. THE BOOK CONTAINS SEVEN FULL-PAGE AND THREE SMALLER PEN AND INK ILLUSTRATIONS BY THE FAMOUS ARTIST E. McKNIGHT KAUFFER. FIRST PUBLISHED IN 1855, FIVE YEARS BEFORE THE START OF THE CIVIL WAR, BENITO CERENO IS A DISTURBING STORY THAT ANALYZES THE RELATIONSHIP BETWEEN WHITE MASTERS AND BLACK AFRICAN SLAVES.

"Herman Melville Memorial Room," furnishing it with Melville's furniture, pictures, and personal belongings.

Thus, Melville, who died in obscurity, has risen to the ranks of the most eminent American writers. Throughout the twentieth century and into the twenty-first, readers have rediscovered the greatness of Herman Melville's writings that was felt by an 1889 admirer, William Clark Russell: "There is no name in American letters that deserves to stand higher [than Melville's] for beauty of imagination, for accuracy of reproduction, for originality of conception, and for a quality of imagination that in 'Moby Dick,' for instance, lifts some of his utterances to such a height of bold and swelling fancy as one must search the pages of the Elizabethan dramatists to parallel" (quoted in Metcalf, 274). To these words, many current readers respond, "Amen."

Works

Novels
Typee: A Peep at Polynesian Life (1846)
Omoo: A Narrative of Adventures in the South Seas (1847)
Mardi and the Voyage Thither (1849)
Redburn: His First Voyage, Being the Sailor-boy Confessions and Reminiscences of the Son-of-a-Gentleman, in the Merchant Service (1849)
White-Jacket; or, The World in a Man-of-War (1850)
Moby Dick; or, The Whale (1851)
Pierre; or, the Ambiguities (1852)
Israel Potter: His Fifty Years of Exile (1855)
The Confidence-Man: His Masquerade (1857)
Billy Budd, Sailor (An Inside Narrative) (1924)

Short Stories
The Piazza Tales (1856)
"The Piazza"
"Bartleby, the Scrivener"
"Benito Cereno"
"The Lightning-Rod Man"
"The Encantadas, or Enchanted Isles"
"The Bell-Tower"

Poetry
Battle-Pieces and Aspects of the War (1866)
Clarel: A Poem and Pilgrimage in the Holy Land (1876)
John Marr and Other Sailors with Some Sea-Pieces (1888)
Timoleon Etc. (1891)
Weeds and Wildings Chiefly: with a Rose or Two (1924)

Journals and Letters

Journal Up the Straits, October 11, 1856-May 5, 1857 (1935)
Republished as *Journal of a Visit to Europe and the Levant,* October 11, 1856-May 6, 1857 *(1955)*
Journal of a Visit to London and the Continent by Herman Melville, 1849–1850 (1948)
The Letters of Herman Melville (1960)

Filmography

So many films have been made of Melville's life, we don't have space to list all. Below is a list of the more accessible titles.

Bartleby. Dir. Jonathan Parker. With Crispin Glover and David Paymer. 2001.

Bartleby. Dir. Anthony Friedman. With Paul Scofield and John McEnery. 1970.

Billy Budd. Television Opera. Music by Benjamin Britten. Libretto by Eric Crozier and E. M. Forster. With Dwayne Croft and James Morris. 1998.

Billy Budd. Dir. Peter Ustinov. With Terence Stamp, Peter Ustinov, and Robert Ryan. 1962.

Enchanted Island. Dir. Allan Dwan. With Jane Powell, Dana Andrews, Don Dubbins, Arthur Shields, Frederick Ledebur. 1958.

Moby Dick. USA Television Miniseries. Dir. Franc Roddam. With Patrick Stewart and Gregory Peck. 1998.

Moby Dick. Dir. John Huston. With Gregory Peck, Richard Basehart, and Orson Welles. 1956

Pola X. (Fr.) Dir. Leos Carax. With Guillaume Depardieu. 1993

Background and Criticism
These films are nonfictional discussions of the *Moby Dick* legend.

Moby Dick. Discovery University Production. Films for the Humanities and Sciences. 2004. Includes dramatizations, film clips, and commentary. *From Fact to Fiction: Moby Dick*. Discovery Channel School. 2003.

Moby Dick: The True Story. Dir. Christopher Rowley. 2002.

Revenge of the Whale. Television Documentary. Dir. Geoff Stephens. With Liam Neeson. 2001.

History's Mysteries: The Essex—The True Story of Moby Dick. Television. The History Channel. 2001.

Chronology

1819
August 1: Herman Melvill is born in New York City to Allan and Maria Melvill

1826–1830
Attends New York Male High School and Columbia Grammar School

1830
October: Allan Melvill's import business fails; the family moves to Albany; Herman becomes a student at the Albany Academy

1832
January 28: Father, Allan Melvill, dies, heavily in debt
March (?): Mother, Maria, changes family's last name to Melville

1832–1837
Herman is taken out of school and works to support family

1835
Enters Albany Classical School

1837
April 15: Brother Gansevoort's fur business fails
Fall: Herman teaches school near Pittsfield, Massachusetts

1838
May: The Melvilles move from Albany to Lansingburgh,
New York
November: Enrolls at Lansingburgh Academy

1839
June 5: Sails to Liverpool, England, as a cabin boy on the
St. Lawrence
September 30: Returns to New York City
Fall: Teaches at Greenbush, New York

1840
May: Teaches at Brunswick, New York
June: Travels west with friend Eli Fly in search of a job

1841
January 3: Sails as a common seaman on the whaler
Acushnet

1842
July 9: Deserts ship, spends a month with the inhabitants
of the Taipi Valley
August 9: Escapes from the natives and joins the
Australian whaler *Lucy Ann*
September: Is involved in a crew rebellion and is briefly
imprisoned in Tahiti
October: Escapes to the island of Eimeo and works as a
farmhand
November: Joins the crew of the Nantucket whaler
Charles and Henry

1843
May 2: Lands in Maui. Goes to Honolulu and works at
odd jobs
August 17: Signs as a seaman aboard the frigate *United
States*

1844
October: Returns to Boston and is discharged from the Navy

1844–1845
Winter: Begins writing about his adventures

1846
Winter: *Typee* is published (February in London; March 17 in New York)

1847
Spring: *Omoo* is published
August 4: Marries Elizabeth Shaw and settles in New York City

1849
February 6: First child, Malcolm, is born
Spring: *Mardi* is published
November: *Redburn* is published

1850
March: *White-Jacket* is published
Summer: Purchases and moves to Arrowhead, a farm near Pittsfield, MA
August 5: Forms a friendship with neighbor Nathaniel Hawthorne
1851
October 22: Second son, Stanwix, is born
Fall: *Moby Dick* is published

1852
Summer: *Pierre* is published

1853
May 22: First daughter, Elizabeth (Bessie), is born

1853–1856
Wrote stories and sketches for magazines, including "Bartleby, the Scrivener"

1855
March 2: Second daughter, Frances, is born
Israel Potter is published in book form, after serialization in *Putnam's*

1856
May: *The Piazza Tales* is published
October 11: Begins traveling in Europe, Egypt, and the Holy Lands to try to recover from physical and mental near collapse

1857
April 1: *The Confidence-Man* is published
May 5: Sails for New York

1857–1860
Earns money as a traveling lecturer

1860
May: Sails around Cape Horn to San Francisco with seafaring brother
November 12: Returns home

1863
Fall: Sells Arrowhead and returns to New York City

1866
August: *Battle-Pieces and Aspects of the War* is published
December 5: Appointed a district inspector of customs, New York harbor

1867
May: Lizzie discusses a legal separation from Herman
September 11: Son Malcolm dies of a self-inflicted pistol
wound

1876
June: *Clarel* is published

1885
December 31: Resigns position as customs inspector

1886
February: Son Stanwix dies in California

1888
March: Takes trip to Bermuda and Florida
John Marr and Other Sailors is privately printed
Begins writing *Billy Budd*

1891
May: *Timoleon* is privately printed
September 28: Dies of a heart attack at age 72

1924
Billy Budd is published posthumously

Notes

Chapter 1

p. 10, Many biographers write that Allan Melvill suffered a nervous breakdown and died insane. Letters written by Allan's brother, Thomas, suggest this. However, based on present-day knowledge of sicknesses, Melville's grand-daughter claims that his delirium was more likely brought on by pneumonia than an unstable emotional state. Melville Metcalf, *Herman Melville*

p. 12, par. 3, Melville's notes written at the time provide detailed information about his first sea voyage. See Leyda, ed., *The Melville Log*, 86–96.

p. 13, par. 1, For more information on the dangers of whaling, see Leyda, 1:115; Delbanco, *Melville*, 40; Robertson-Lorant, *Melville*, 96–99.

p. 15, par. 2, Walt Whitman, Brooklyn *Eagle*, 15 April 1846; in Leyda, 1:211.

p. 15, par. 3, "thorough entertainment": Brooklyn *Eagle*, 5 May 1847; in Leyda, 1:243.

p. 16, par. 2, "equal to its predecessor": London *Spectator*, 10 April 1847; in Parker, *Herman Melville*, 503.

p. 17, par. 2, The Melville family always helped Herman get his works published. The women often spent months making the copy for the publisher, and they helped correct the proof sheets. Leyda, 1:276; Mumford, *Herman Melville*, 91; Robertson-Lorant, 170, 239; and Parker, 1:612; for more on the sisters' involvement see Parker 2:208, 227, 242–245, 441, 461, and Metcalf, 154.

p. 17, par. 3, *Southern Literary Messenger*, December 1849; in Leyda, 1:355.

p. 18, par. 4, "as perfect a specimen": London *Literary Gazette*, 20 October 1849; in Leyda, 1:322.

"disposed to place a higher value": *Bentley's Miscellany*, [1] November 1849; in Leyda, 1:324.

p. 19, par. 1, *Bentley's Miscellany*, March 1850; in Parker, 1:715.

p. 20, par. 2, For more information on the books Melville studied as he was composing *Moby Dick*, see Parker, 1:695–696.

p. 22, par. 2, "trash of conception": Boston *Post*, July 1852; in Leyda, 1:455.

"a dead failure": New York *Albion*, 21 August, 1852; in Parker, 2:128.

"HERMAN MELVILLE CRAZY": *New York Day Book*, 7 September 1852; in Parker 2:131-132.

"gone 'clean daft'": *Southern Quarterly Review*, October 1852; in Leyda, 1:463.

p. 23, par. 2, *Berkshire County Eagle*, 30 May 1856; in Leyda, 2:515.

p. 24, par. 3, "curious, spirited, and well worth reading": Philadelphia *Daily Evening Bulletin*, 11 April 1857; in Parker, 2:350.

"has not the slightest qualifications": New York *Evening Times*, 11 April 1857; in Leyda, 2:570.

p. 29, par. 1, *Nation*, 6 September 1866; in Leyda, 2:683.

p. 29, par. 2, Melville's granddaughter felt $4.00 per day was excellent pay; she called it a "munificent salary" (Metcalf, 206). According to labor analyst Bruce Laurie, a salary of $1,200 per year in nineteenth-century America would have been a high wage. Laurie, *Artisans into Workers*, 59; 633.

p. 30, par. 5, New York *Independent*, 6 July 1876; in Parker, 2:805.

p. 31, par. 1, *Clarel* took a great deal of time. In a letter dated February 2, 1857, Lizzie says, "The book is going through the press, and every minute of Herman's time and mine is devoted to it—the mere mechanical work of reading proof &c is so great and absorbing." In this same letter she also remarks on Herman's "frightfully nervous state" and begs relatives, even Herman's sisters, not to visit. (quoted in Leyda, 2:746-747).

p. 35, par, 3, *New York Press*; 29 September 1891, in Leyda, 2:836.

Chapter 3

Throughout the manuscript, all references to *Typee* are from Herman Melville. *Typee: A Peep at Polynesian Life.* Intro. by Robert Sullivan. New York: Modern Library, 2001.

p. 50, par. 1, Although almost all critics interpret "lover of human flesh" to be "eater" of human flesh, Toni H. Oliviero argues that the words could also refer to sexuality. She sees the Typees as humans who not only love to eat the human body but also sexually enjoy the human body. Oliviero, "Ambiguous Utopia," 39–40.

p. 50, par. 3, "Freshness and originality": London *Times*, 6 April 1846; in Leyda, ed., *The Melville Log*, 1:210.

"Animation and vivacity": *United States Magazine* and *Democratic Review*, May 1846; in Leyda, 1:216.

"Easy, gossiping style": The *Knickerbocker*, May 1846; in Leyda, 1:216.

Nathaniel Hawthorne: Salem *Advertiser*, 25 March, 1846; in Leyda, 1:207.

Walt Whitman: *Brooklyn Eagle*, 15 April, 1846; in Leyda, 1:211.

p. 50, par. 4, *Morning Courier* and *New-York Enquirer*, 17 April 1846; in Leyda, 1:211.

p. 51, par. 2, *Christian Parlor Magazine*, July 1846; in Leyda, 1:225.

The American Review, April 1846; in Leyda, 1:212.

"voluptuous": *American Review*, July 1847; in Parker, *Herman Melville*, 1:532.

"perverse": *The New Englander*, July 1846; in Leyda, 1: 225.

Chapter 4

Throughout the manuscript, all references to *Moby Dick* are from Herman Melville, *Moby Dick; or, The Whale,* edited with introduction and notes by Tony Tanner, (Oxford: Oxford University Press, 1988; reissued, 1998). p. 53–54, Melville based the *Pequod*'s destruction by Moby Dick on a true story. In 1820 the Nantucket whaler *Essex* was sunk when a huge sperm whale attacked it twice. An account of the *Essex*'s story can be found in Nathaniel Philbrick, *In the Heart of the Sea.*

p. 63, par. 2, Editor Tony Tanner explains that the Heidelburgh Tun is "a wine cask in the castle of Heidelberg with a capacity of 49,000 gallons" (*Moby Dick*, 304n; 523)

p. 88, par. 3, "far beyond the level of an ordinary work of fiction" with its "true philosophy," "genuine poetry," and "profound reflections": *John Bull*, 25 October 1851; in Leyda, ed., *The Melville Log*, 1:431.

"trash belonging to the worst school of Bedlam literature": London *Athenæum*, 25 October 1851; in Leyda, 1:430–431. "not worth the money asked for it, either as a literary work or as a mass of printed paper": Boston Post, 20 November 1851; in Parker, *Herman Melville*, 20.

"piratical running down of creeds and opinions": *The Literary World*, 22 Nov. 1851; in Leyda, 1:437.

"The Judgment day will hold him liable for not turning his talents to better account": New York *Independent*, 20 November 1851; in Parker, 2: 25.

"with the gusto of true genius" and "the raciness of his humor and the redolence of his imagination": Morning *Courier* and New York *Enquirer*, 14 November 1851; in Leyda, 1: 434.

Chapter 6
Throughout the manuscript, all references to *Billy Budd, Sailor (An Inside Narrative): Reading Text and Genetic Text* are from Harrison Hayford and Merton Sealts Jr., eds. Chicago: University of Chicago Press, 1962.
p. 109, par. 2, The phrase "testament of acceptance" was coined in 1933 by E. L. Grant Watson who boldly asserted that "Melville is no longer a rebel." E. L. Grant Watson, "Melville's Testament of Acceptance," in *Melville's* Billy Budd *and the Critics*, ed. William T. Stafford (San Francisco: Wadsworth, 1961), 76.

Further Information

Further Reading

Delbanco, Andrew. *Melville: His World and Work*. New York: Alfred A. Knopf, 2005.

Hardwick, Elizabeth. *Herman Melville*. New York: Viking, 2000.

Leyda, Jay, ed. *The Melville Log: A Documentary Life of Herman Melville, 1819–1891*. vol. 1: 1819-1854; vol. 2: 1855–1891. New York: Harcourt, Brace, 1951. Reprint, New York: Gordian Press, 1969.

Parker, Hershel. *Herman Melville: A Biography*. vol. 1: 1819–1851; vol. 2: 1851–1891. Baltimore: Johns Hopkins University Press, 1996, 2002.

Robertson-Lorant, Laurie. *Melville: A Biography*. Amherst: University of Massachusetts Press, 1996.

Web Sites

Bibliomania: Herman Melville
http://www.bibliomania.com/0/0/36frameset.html
Has many of Melville's novels and short stories available
to read online.

Hawthorne in Salem
http://www.hawthorneinsalem.org
Relates to Herman Melville and Nathaniel Hawthorne

Herman Melville
http://people.brandeis.edu/~teuber/melvillebio.html
Includes a biography, discussion of Melville's genres, further readings about Melville, and information on *Typee*, *Omoo*, *Moby Dick*, *Pierre*, *Billy Budd*, "Bartleby," and others

Herman Melville
http://www.poets.org
Features news, works, and life of Herman Melville

Herman Melville's Arrowhead
http://www.mobydick.org
Contains information on Herman Melville's Arrowhead

Bibliography

The following is a selection of the material the author found especially helpful in her research.

Works by Melville

Melville, Herman. "Bartleby, the Scrivener: A Story of Wall-Street." In *Piazza Tales and Other Prose Pieces 1839-1860*, edited by Harrison Hayford, Alma A. MacDougall, and G. Thomas Tanselle. 13–45. Evanston and Chicago: Northwestern University Press and the Newberry Library, 1987.

————. Billy Budd, Sailor (*An Inside Narrative*): *Reading Text and Genetic Text*. Edited by Harrison Hayford and Merton Sealts Jr. Chicago: University of Chicago Press, 1962.

————. *Collected Poems of Herman Melville*. Edited by Howard P. Vincent. Chicago: Packard and Co., Henricks House, 1947.

————. *The Confidence-Man, His Masquerade*. Edited by Harrison Hayford, Hershel Parker, and G. Thomas Tanselle. Evanston and Chicago: Northwestern University Press and the Newberry Library, 1984.

————. *Israel Potter: His Fifty Years in Exile*. Edited by Harrison Hayford, Hershel Parker, and G. Thomas Tanselle. Evanston and Chicago: Northwestern University Press and the Newberry Library, 1982.

———. *Moby Dick; or, The Whale*. Edited with introduction and notes by Tony Tanner. Oxford: Oxford University Press, 1988. Reissued, 1998.

———. *Omoo: A Narrative of Adventures in the South Seas*. Edited by Harrison Hayford, Hershel Parker, and G. Thomas Tanselle. Evanston and Chicago: Northwestern University Press and the Newberry Library, 1968.

———. *Piazza Tales and Other Prose Pieces 1839–1860*. Edited by Harrison Hayford, Alma A. MacDougall, and G. Thomas Tanselle. Evanston and Chicago: Northwestern University Press and the Newberry Library, 1987.

———. *Pierre; or, the Ambiguities*. Introduction and notes by William C. Spengemann. New York: Penguin Books, 1996.

———. *Redburn: His First Voyage, Being the Sailor-boy Confessions and Reminiscences of the Son-of-a-Gentleman, in the Merchant Service*. Edited by Harrison Hayford, Hershel Parker, and G. Thomas Tanselle. Evanston and Chicago: Northwestern University Press and the Newberry Library, 1969.

———. *Typee: A Peep at Polynesian Life*. Introduction by Robert Sullivan. New York: Modern Library, 2001.

———. *White-Jacket, or The World in a Man-of-War*. Edited by Harrison Hayford, Hershel Parker, and G. Thomas Tanselle. Evanston and Chicago: Northwestern University Press and the Newberry Library, 1970.

Works about Melville

Adler, Joyce Sparer. *War in Melville's Imagination*. New York: New York University Press, 1981.

Auden, W. H. *The Enchafèd Flood: or the Romantic Iconography of the Sea.* New York: Random House, 1950.

———. "Herman Melville." In *Twentieth Century Interpretations of Billy Budd.* Edited by Howard P. Vincent. Englewood Cliffs, NJ: Prentice-Hall, 1971 105–106.

Bezanson, Walter E. "Moby-Dick: Work of Art." In *Moby-Dick: An Authoritative Text.* Edited by Hershel Parker and Harrison Hayford. 2nd ed. New York: W. W. Norton, 2002: 641–657.

Bickley, R. Bruce, Jr. *The Method of Melville's Short Fiction.* Durham, NC: Duke University Press, 1975.

Blair, Walter, et al., ed. *American Literature: A Brief History.* Revised ed. Glenview, IL: Scott, Foresman, 1974. Casper, Leonard. "The Case Against Captain Vere." In Stafford, ed. *Melville's Billy Budd and the Critics.* Edited by William T. Stafford, San Francisco: Wadsworth Publishing, 1961, 153–155.

Coffler, Gail. "Religion, Myth, and the Meaning in the Art of Billy Budd, Sailor." In *New Essays on Billy Budd.* Edited by Donald Yannella. Cambridge, MA: Cambridge University Press, 2002, 49–82.

Cook, Charles H. Jr. "Ahab's 'Intolerable Allegory.'" In *Discussions of Moby-Dick.* Edited by Milton R. Stern. Boston: D.C. Heath, 1960, 60–65.

Cook, Reginald L. "Big Medicine in Moby Dick." In *Discussions of Moby-Dick.* Edited by Milton R. Stern. Boston: D.C. Heath, 1960, 60–65. 19–24.

Craver, Donald H. and Patricia R. Plante. "Bartleby, or, the Ambiguities." *Studies in Short Fiction* 20 (Spring-Summer 1983), 132–136.

Davis, Todd F. "The Narrator's Dilemma in 'Bartleby the Scrivener': The Excellently Illustrated Re-statement of a Problem." *Studies in Short Fiction* 34 (1997), 183–192.

Delbanco, Andrew. *Melville: His World and Work.* New York: Alfred A. Knopf, 2005.

Dilworth, Thomas. "Narrator of 'Bartleby': The Christian-Humanist Acquaintance of John Jacob Astor." *Papers on Language and Literature* 38, no.1 (Winter 2002), 49–75.

Doloff, Steven. "The Prudent Samaritan: Melville's 'Bartleby, the Scrivener' as Parody of Christ's Parable to the Lawyer." *Studies in Short Fiction* 34 (1997), 357–361.

Dumm, Thomas L. "Who Is Ishmael?" *Massachusetts Review* 46.3 (September 2005), 398–414.

Eitner, Walter H. "The Lawyer's Rockaway Trips in 'Bartleby, the Scrivener.'" *Melville Society Extracts* 78 (September 1989), 14–16.

Evans, Lyon Jr. "'Too Good to be True': Subverting Christian Hope in Billy Budd." *New England Quarterly* 15 (September 1982), 323–353.

Farmer, Philip José. *The Wind Whales of Ishmael.* New York: Penguin/Ace Books, 1971.

Faulkner, William. ["I Wish I Had Written That."] In *Moby-Dick: An Authoritative Text.* 2nd ed. Edited by Hershel Parker and Harrison Hayford. New York: W. W. Norton, 2002, 640.

Foley, Barbara. "From Wall Street to Astor Place: Historicizing Melville's 'Bartleby.'" *American Literature* 72.1 (March 2000), 87–116.

Forster, E. M. *Aspects of the Novel.* New York: Harcourt Brace Jovanovich, 1929.

Franklin, H. Bruce. "Herman Melville: Artist of the Worker's World." In *Weapons of Criticism: Marxism in American and the Literary Tradition.* Edited by Norman Rudich. Palo Alto, CA: Ramparts Press, 1976, 287–309.

———. *The Victim as Criminal and Artist.* New York: Oxford University Press, 1978.

———. *The Wake of the Gods: Melville's Mythology.* Stanford: Stanford University Press, 1963.

Garner, Stanton. "Fraud as Fact in Herman Melville's *Billy Budd.*" *San Jose Studies* 4 (May 1978), 82–105.

Garrison, Joseph Jr. "Billy Budd: A Reconsideration." *Ball Sate University Forum* 27 (1986), 30–41.

Gilmore, Michael T. *American Romanticism and the Marketplace. Chicago:* University of Chicago Press, 1985.

———, ed. *Twentieth Century Interpretations of Moby-Dick: A Collection of Critical Essays.* Englewood Cliffs, NJ: Prentice-Hall, 1977.

Glick, Wendell. "Expediency and Absolute Morality in *Billy Budd*." In *Melville's Billy Budd and the Critics.* Edited by William T. Stafford. San Francisco: Wadsworth Publishing, 1961, 104–111.

Greenberg, Martin. "The Difficult Justice of Melville and Kleist." *New Criterion* 23, no. 7 (March 2005), 24–32. Hardwick, Elizabeth. *Herman Melville.* New York: Viking, 2000.

Harvey, Bruce A. "'Precepts Graven on Every Breast': Melville's *Typee* and the Forms of the Law." *American Quarterly* 45, no. 3 (September 1993), 394–424.

Hayford, Harrison. "'Loomings': Yarns and Figures in the Fabric." In *Moby-Dick: An Authoritative Text.* 2nd ed. Edited by Hershel Parker and Harrison Hayford. New York: W. W. Norton, 2002, 657–669.

Hetherington, Hugh D. "Early Reviews of Moby-Dick." In *Discussions of Moby-Dick.* Edited by Milton R. Stern. Boston: D.C. Heath, 1960, 1–18.

Hillway, Tyrus. *Herman Melville.* New York: Twayne Publishers, 1963.

Hoag, Ronald Wesley. "The Corpse in the Office: Mortality, Mutability, and Salvation in 'Bartleby, the Scrivener.'" *ESQ* 38 (1992), 119–142.

Hunt, Lester H. "*Billy Budd*: Melville's Dilemma." *Philosophy and Literature* 26, no.2 (2002), 273–295.

Ivison, Douglas. "'I Saw Everything But Could Comprehend Nothing': Melville's *Typee*, Travel Narrative, and Colonial Discourse." *American Transcendental Quarterly* 16, no. 2 (June 2002), 115–130.

Jehlen, M., ed. *Herman Melville: A Collection of Critical Essays.* Vol. 4. New York: Prentice, 1994.

John, Richard R. "The Lost World of Bartleby, the Ex-Officeholder: Variations on a Venerable Literary Form."

New England Quarterly 70, no. 4 (December 1997), 631–641.

Karcher, Carolyn. *Shadow Over the Promised Land: Slavery, Race, and Violence in Melville's America.* Baton Rouge: Louisiana State University Press, 1980.

Kazin, Alfred. "An Introduction to Moby-Dick." In *Discussions of Moby-Dick.* Edited by Milton R. Stern. Boston: D.C. Heath, 1960, 52–59.

Kearns, Michael. "Melville's Chaotic Style and the Use of Generative Models: An Essay in Method." *Style* 30, no. 1 (Spring 1996), 50–68.

Laurie, Bruce. *Artisans into Workers: Labor in Nineteenth-Century America.* New York: Farrar, Straus and Giroux, 1989.

Lewis, R. W. B. *The American Adam: Innocence, Tragedy and Tradition in the Nineteenth Century.* Chicago: University of Chicago Press, 1955.

Leyda, Jay, ed. *The Melville Log: A Documentary Life of Herman Melville, 1819–1891.* Vol. 1: 1819–1854; Vol. 2: 1855–1891. New York: Harcourt, Brace, 1951. Reprint, New York: Gordian Press, 1969.

Loges, Max L. "Melville's Billy Budd." *Explicator* 55.3 (Spring 1997), 137–138.

McCall, Dan. *The Silence of Bartleby*. Ithaca, NY: Cornell University Press, 1989.

Metcalf, Eleanor Melville. *Herman Melville: Cycle and Epicycle*. Cambridge, MA: Harvard University Press, 1953.

Milder, Robert, ed. "Introduction [and] Explanatory Notes," in *Billy Budd, Sailor and Selected Tales*. vii–xli, 375-410. Oxford: Oxford University Press, 1998.

Miller, James E. Jr. *A Reader's Guide to Herman Melville*. New York: Farrar, Straus and Giroux, 1962.

Mitchell, Thomas. "Dead Letters and Dead Men: Narrative Purpose in 'Bartleby the Scrivener.'" *Studies in Short Fiction* 27 (Summer 1990), 329–338.

Morgan, Winifred. "'Bartleby' and the Failure of Conventional Virtue." *Renascence* 45.4 (Summer 1993), 257–271.

Mumford, Lewis. H*erman Melville: A Study of His Life and Vision*. New York: Harcourt, Brace and World, 1929.

Murry, John Middleton. ["From John Middleton Murry (1924)."] In *Melville's Billy Budd and the Critics*. Edited by William T. Stafford. San Francisco: Wadsworth Publishing, 1961, 69–70.

Naslund, Sena Jeter. *Ahab's Wife: Or, the Star Gazer*. New York: William Morrow/Harper Collins, 1999.

Oates, Joyce Carol. "Melville and the Tragedy of Nihilism." *Texas Studies in Literature and Language* 4 (Spring 1962), 59–83.

Oliviero, Toni H. "Ambiguous Utopia: Savagery and Civilization in Typee and Omoo." *Modern Language Studies* 13, no. 1 (Winter 1983), 39–46.

Parker, Hershel. "Billy Budd, Foretopman and the Dynamics of Canonization." *College Literature* 17, no. 1 (February 1990), 21–32.

————. *Herman Melville: A Biography.* Vol. 1: 1819–1851; Vol. 2: 1851–1891. Baltimore: Johns Hopkins University Press, 1996, 2002.

———— and Harrison Hayford., ed. *Moby-Dick: An Authoritative Text.* 2nd ed. New York: W. W. Norton, 2002.

Philbrick, Nathaniel. *In the Heart of the Sea: The Tragedy of the Whaleship Essex.* New York: Penguin, 2000.

Phillips, Kathy J. "Billy Budd as Anti-Homophobic Text." *College English* 56 (1994), 896–910.

Reed, Naomi D. "The Specter of Wall Street: 'Bartleby, the Scrivener' and the Language of Commodities." *American Literature* 76, no. 2 (June 2004), 247–273.

Reeves, John D. *Windows on Melville.* Danbury, CT: Rutledge Books, 2001.

Reno, Janet. *Ishmael Alone Survived.* Lewisburg, PA: Bucknell University Press, 1990.

Reynolds, Larry J. "Billy Budd and American Labor Unrest: The Case for Striking Back." In *New Essays on*

Billy Budd. Edited by Donald Yannella. Cambridge, MA: Cambridge University Press, 2002, 21–48.

Robertson-Lorant, Laurie. *Melville: A Biography.* Amherst: University of Massachusetts Press, 1996.

Weeds and Wildings Chiefly: with a Rose or Two, by Herman Melville: Reading Text and Genetic Text. Edited with introduction by Robert Charles Ryan. Evanston, IL: Northwestern University Press, 1967.

Schippe, Cullen and Chuck Stetson, eds. *The Bible and Its Influence.* New York: BLP Publishing, 2006.

Sedgwick, Eve. K. "Billy Budd: After the Homosexual." In *Herman Melville: A Collection of Critical Essays.* Vol. 4. Edited by M. Jehlen. 217–234. New York: Prentice, 1994.

Silver, Alan. "The Lawyer and the Scrivener." *Partisan Review* 47 (1981), 409–424.

Stone, Geoffrey. ["Claggart—II."] In *Melville's Billy Budd and the Critics.* Edited by William T. Stafford. San Francisco: Wadsworth Publishing, 1961, 159–160.

Sullivan, Robert. "Introduction." *Typee: A Peep at Polynesian Life.* Herman Melville. New York: Modern Library, 2001, xiii–xvi.

Swann, Charles. "Dating the Action of 'Bartleby.'" *Notes and Queries* 32 (September 1985), 357–358.

Thomas, Brook. *Cross-Examinations of Law and Literature.* Cambridge, MA: Cambridge University Press, 1987.

Verne, Jules. *20,000 Leagues Under the Sea*. 1870. Reprint, New York: Thomas A. Barron, 1995.

Weinstock, Jeffrey Andrew. "Doing Justice to Bartleby." *American Transcendental Quarterly* 17.1 (March 2003), 23–42.

Wenke, John. "Melville's Indirection: Billy Budd, The Genetic Text, and 'The Deadly Space Between.'" In *New Essays on Billy Budd*. Edited by Donald Yanella. Cambridge, MA: Cambridge University Press, 2002, 114–144.

Widmer, Kingsley. *The Ways of Nihilism: A Study of Herman Melville's Short Novels*. Los Angeles: Ward-Ritchie Press, 1970.

Wilson, James C. "'Bartleby': The Walls of Wall Street." *Arizona Quarterly* 37 (Winter 1981), 335–346.

Withim, Phil. "'Billy Budd': Testament of Resistance." In *Melville's Billy Budd and the Critics*. Edited by William T. Stafford. San Francisco: Wadsworth Publishing, 1961, 78–90.

Wood, James. *The Broken Estate*. New York: Random House, 1999.

Yannella, Donald, ed. "Introduction" in *New Essays on Billy Budd*. Cambridge, MA: Cambridge University Press, 2002, 1–20.

Yoder, Jonathan A. "The Protagonists' Rainbow in Billy Budd: Critical Trimming of Truth's Ragged Edges." *American Transcendental Quarterly* 7, no. 2 (June 1993), 98–114.

Index

About the Author

Raychel Haugrud Reiff, a professor of English at the University of Wisconsin-Superior, has published fifteen articles on literary topics and effective teaching techniques in various journals and books. Her books in Marshall Cavendish Benchmark's Writers and Their Works series are *Herman Melville: Moby Dick and Other Works* and *Charlotte Brontë: Jane Eyre and Villette*. She lives in Superior, Wisconsin.